The True Dream

The True Dream is a Persian satirical drama set in Isfahan in the lead up to Iran's Constitutional Revolution of 1905–11. Although its three authors hail from the clerical class, they criticize the arrogance, corruption and secularity of the Iranian ruling dynasty and clergy, taking Isfahan as their example. The work blends fact and fiction by summoning the prominent men of the city to account for themselves on the Day of Judgement. God speaks offstage, delivering withering judgements of their behaviour. The dream of the authors is a vision of an Iran governed by law, where justice prevails and the clergy are honestly religious.

This book has the Persian and English translation on facing pages. The introduction presents brief biographies of the authors – who wrote anonymously, but were all executed. One of the authors was the father of Mohammad-Ali Jamâlzâdeh, a pioneer of modern Persian fiction, and *The True Dream* was one of the first dramas, in European style, to be written in Persian. The book shows that today's struggle for a modern society began more than a century ago, and then and now pivots on the role of the Islamic clerics (the ulama).

Using colloquial language, this first English translation of a significant and humorous Persian satirical drama will prove an accessible and valuable resource for students of Persian. By marking a significant point in the influence of Western political philosophy and Western drama on the Persian intellectual classes, this book will also appeal to students and scholars of Middle Eastern History and Political Science.

Ali-Asghar Seyed-Gohrab is Associate Professor at Leiden University. He has authored a wide range of books, articles and translations in the field of Persian Studies and Islamic Spirituality and Mysticism (Sufism).

Sen McGlinn is a student of religion and a translator, with a particular focus on religion and politics in Iran in the modern period. He writes on Bahai Theology and related topics.

Iranian Studies
Edited by Homa Katouzian
University of Oxford
Mohamad Tavakoli
University of Toronto

Since 1967 the International Society for Iranian Studies (ISIS) has been a leading learned society for the advancement of new approaches in the study of Iranian society, history, culture, and literature. The new ISIS Iranian Studies series published by Routledge will provide a venue for the publication of original and innovative scholarly works in all areas of Iranian and Persianate Studies.

29 The Historiography of Persian Architecture
Edited by Mohammad Gharipour

30 Iran and Russian Imperialism
The Ideal Anarchists, 1800–1914
Moritz Deutschmann

31 Iranian Music and Popular Entertainment
From *Motrebi* to *Losanjelesi* and beyond
GJ Breyley and Sasan Fatemi

32 Gender and Dance in Iran
Biopolitics on the twentieth-century stage
Ida Meftahi

33 Persian Authorship and Canonicity in Late Mughal Delhi
Building an ark
Prashant Keshavmurthy

34 Iran and the Nuclear Question
History and the evolutionary trajectory
Mohammad Homayounvash

35 The True Dream
An English translation with facing Persian text
Ali-Asghar Seyed-Gohrab and Sen McGlinn

The True Dream
Indictment of the Shiite clerics of Isfahan, an English translation with facing Persian text

Seyyed Jamâl-al-Din Wâʿez
Malek-al-Motakallemin
Sheykh Ahmad Kermâni
edited by Ali-Asghar Seyed-Gohrab and Sen McGlinn

LONDON AND NEW YORK

First published 2017
by Routledge
2 Park Square, Milton Park, Abingdon, Oxon OX14 4RN

and by Routledge
711 Third Avenue, New York, NY 10017

Routledge is an imprint of the Taylor & Francis Group, an informa business

© 2017 Ali-Asghar Seyed-Gohrab and Sen McGlinn

The right of Ali-Asghar Seyed-Gohrab and Sen McGlinn to be identified as editors of this work has been asserted by them in accordance with sections 77 and 78 of the Copyright, Designs and Patents Act 1988.

All rights reserved. No part of this book may be reprinted or reproduced or utilised in any form or by any electronic, mechanical, or other means, now known or hereafter invented, including photocopying and recording, or in any information storage or retrieval system, without permission in writing from the publishers.

Trademark notice: Product or corporate names may be trademarks or registered trademarks, and are used only for identification and explanation without intent to infringe.

British Library Cataloguing in Publication Data
A catalogue record for this book is available from the British Library

Library of Congress Cataloguing in Publication Data
A catalog record for this book has been requested

ISBN: 978-1-138-22372-1 (hbk)
ISBN: 978-1-315-40390-8 (ebk)

Typeset in Times New Roman
by Swales & Willis Ltd, Exeter, Devon, UK

Printed in the United Kingdom
by Henry Ling Limited

Contents

Introduction 1

Seyyed Jamâl-al-Din Wâ'ez Esfahâni 3
A sermon by Seyyed Jamâl-al-Din 6
Seyyed Mirzâ Nasrollâh Beheshti (Malek-al-Motakallemin) 14
Hâjj Mirzâ Ahmad Kermâni (Majd al-Eslâm) 16
The plot of The True Dream *18*
History of the text and publications 19
The book's literary merits 19
Works cited 21

***

Translation of *The True Dream* 24

Appendix: The True Dream *in Malekzâde's* History
of the Iranian Constitutional Revolution   128
Notes   132
Index   139

Introduction

The book translated here is a remarkable example of literature's role in modern Persian history, showing in a critical but engaging fashion how Persian intellectuals struggled to limit both the power of the ulamâ and absolute political rule in the decades preceding the Constitutional Revolution (1905–11). The authors are themselves from the clerical class, but were convinced of the pressing need for a new society based on the rule of secular codified laws. They campaigned against despotism, corruption and nepotism and were eloquent orators who could attract large crowds in major Persian cities. They used their positions to disseminate new ideas on social and political reform, championing the ideals of freedom, justice and human rights.

The title of the treatise *Ro'yâ-ye sâdeqe* or *The True Dream* is significant as the term 'true' dream distinguishes it from a 'false' dream. Whereas false dreams come from Satan or from man himself and cannot predict future events, true dreams find their origin in God and can predict future events. True dreams are experienced by true believers, saints and prophets.[1]

The True Dream is written by three men: Seyyed Jamâl-al-Din Wâ'ez, Malek-al-Motakallemin ('King of Orators') and Sheykh Ahmad Kermâni (Majd al-Eslâm). We know little about the process and time of composition of this work but in several secondary works, the names of the authors are attached to *The True Dream*.[2] It depicts the rule of Prince Soltân Mas'ud Mirzâ, known as Zell-al-Soltân ('The Shadow of the King'), and Âqâ Najafi, the senior cleric of the city of Isfahan.[3] Zell-al-Soltân was one of the sons of Nâser-al-Din Shah and the older brother of Mozaffar-al-Din Shah. He governed the southern parts of Persia from Isfahan. Browne says that "the Zillu's-Soltân was hated by the Persians, especially by the Isfahânis, who had the best opportunities of knowing him, on account of his numerous acts of cruelty."[4] His despotism was a byword, especially among the people of Isfahan.[5]

We have several reports from various sources about his treatment of people.[6] One of these sources is Mirzâ Hoseyn-e Âzâd Tabrizi, son of the influential reformer Mirzâ Yusof Khân Mostashâr-al-Dowle (d. 1895). A medical doctor, he studied in London and obtained his *doctorat en médicine* in Paris. He returned to Persia in 1882. Arriving in Tehran, he was advised by Dr. Joséph Desirée

Tholozan, Nâser-al-Din Shah's personal doctor, to become Zell-al-Soltân's physician. De Bruijn states that because of the "humiliating services" Hoseyn-e Âzad had to render at the court, he looked for a chance to leave Persia. One of these humiliations was requiring the doctor to clean the imperial nails before the Court and his European guests.[7] Âzâd left Iran on the pretext of attending the World Exhibition in Paris in 1898. He stayed in Paris and worked at the Bibliothèque Nationale.[8]

Sheykh Mohammad-Taqi Âqâ Najafi is depicted in this book as a short-sighted and ignorant person who does not want to know anything about progress, adhering firmly to the orthodox tenets of Islam. This Âqâ Najafi was a man to be feared. In his memoir, E'temâd-al-Saltane writes that he visited Nâser-al-Din Shah in February 1890, and found the Shah, Zell-al-Soltân and Nâyeb-al-Saltane talking about the troubled situation in Isfahan. On his own initiative, Âqâ Najafi had ordered a number of people to be beheaded, on the accusation of being Bâbis (see below). The king is distressed. Apparently the British Envoy had complained and Âqâ Najafi had to be brought to Tehran.[9] Âqâ Najafi also stirred people to protest against the mighty Zell-al-Soltân.[10] Mohammad-'Ali Jamâlzâde recounts in his memoirs how his school was closed by religious zealots and how, at the order of Âqâ Najafi, the principal Hâji Jawâd was beaten. He reports how Mirzâ Seyyed 'Ali-Naqi's newly founded school, which had a modern curriculum including English, was closed by Âqâ Najafi's followers.[11]

In the closing decades of the nineteenth century, 'Bâbis' were openly tortured and killed across Persia. Bâbism in the proper sense was a messianic movement in Iran and Iraq under the charismatic leadership of Seyyed 'Ali-Mohammad Shirâzi, known as the Bâb, who was executed in 1850. By the late nineteenth century, a large part of the Bâbis had become Bahâ'is, followers of Bahâ'u'llâh (1817–92), while others were known as Azalis, followers of Sobh-e Azal (1830–1912).[12] The Bahâ'i leaders brought a wide range of metaphysical, ethical and exegetical teachings, but they also advocated democracy, constitutional government, the separation of church and state, the education of the masses and an international law and tribunal that would outlaw warfare. A large number of Iran's progressive intellectuals found some of these stances relevant, although in most cases it would be an overstatement to say they converted to the Bahâ'i Faith.[13] The religious teachings of the Bâbis and Bahâ'is marked them quite clearly as heretics from an orthodox Muslim perspective. When intellectuals recognized the virtue of some progressive features of the Bahâ'i programme, conservative activists and propagandists used this as an opportunity to label any advocate of a reform such as a constitution or modern education as a 'Bâbi,' and therefore a heretic and a target in the periodic 'Bâbi-killings.'[14] Two of the authors of *The True Dream* were among those accused of being Bâbis: it is not clear whether they were believers and in sustained contact with the 'Bâbi' (Bahâ'i) community. Short biographies of the authors, presented below, will provide a glimpse of the period and offer some suggestions as to why these liberal men wrote *The True Dream*.

Seyyed Jamâl-al-Din Wâ'ez Esfahâni

Seyyed Jamâl-al-Din Wâ'ez Esfahâni (or Hamadâni, 1862–1908) was the father of Mohammad-'Ali Jamâlzâde (1892–1997), a pioneer of Persian modern fiction.[15] Seyyed Jamâl-al-Din's family came to Isfahan from Lebanon.[16] He was the son of Seyyed 'Isâ Sadr 'Âmeli, a religious jurist in the Dabbâgh-khâne district in Hamadân, whose ancestors go back to Jabal 'Amel in Lebanon. Seyyed Jamâl-al-Din was born in 1863 in Hamadân. When he was five years old, he lost his father, and the family then migrated to Tehran. After several years at school, his mother asked him to work in his maternal uncle's weaving workshop. At the age of fourteen he left the workshop to begin his studies in the traditional Islamic curriculum. At the age of twenty he went to Isfahan, a centre of learning from the sixteenth century, to continue his studies. Here he met our other two authors, Malek-al-Motakallemin and Hâjj Mirzâ Ahmad Kermâni. In Isfahan he pursued his career as a preacher. Having a warm, plain and accessible style of preaching, his career as a preacher thrived. He became one of the best known preachers of Isfahan. As he had contact with Bâbis, it was not long before he was accused of being a Bâbi sympathizer.

Seyyed Jamâl-al-Din was especially effective in conveying ideas of social justice, the rule of law and freedom (defined as the opposite of arbitrary and absolutist rule). He was a very engaged person and participated actively in social and political events. The three authors were among the founders of the Anjoman-e Taraqqi ('Society for Progress') and supported the Islamic Company (*Sherkat-e Eslâmi*), a new textile company founded by the merchant Mohammad-Hoseyn Kâzeruni.[17] The Islamic Company was established after the return of Malek-al-Motakallemin from India. He asked several influential clerics, merchants and government officials to buy shares. Choubine states that in a period in which money was extremely scarce, about nine hundred thousand *tumân* was raised through shares. Afary describes the clerics' relationship with the Islamic Company, as follows:

> Their job was to promote the sale of local textiles and persuade the public not to purchase imported fabrics. They came to enjoy the patronage of the governor, Zell-al-Soltân. Both Zell-al-Soltân and Âqâ Najafi were investors in the new Islamic Company and thus benefited from the preachers' advertising campaigns.[18]

Jamâlzâde writes that his father was made an agent of the company to promote the textiles of Isfahan in Shiraz. He says, "It was decided to pay my mother and me five *tumân*s a month."[19] During these journeys, Seyyed Jamâl-al-Din also preached in the holy months of Moharram and Safar. In Shiraz, Seyyed Jamâl-al-Din also had contact with various prominent figures. Jamâlzâde tells how his father become acquainted with the famous poet of Shiraz, Shuride. The poet even wrote an ode praising his father's qualities. Seyyed Jamâl-al-Din published this ode in a treatise, *Clothes of Piety* (completed 1900), written to promote domestic textiles. The opening lines have been translated as follows:

> His honor, Seyyed Jamâl-od-din, has pure thoughts,
>   Which mirror the virgin beauty of meaning.
> He is a sea in the universe above when he rises to the pulpit,
>   A universe in the boundless sea when he goes in to preach.[20]

As Kashani-Sabet indicates, *Clothes of Piety* "prescribed simple and sensible measures to strengthen the country's economy" as Seyyed-Jamâl-al-Din believed that need (*ihtiyâj*) brings disaster to human beings.[21] Seyyed-Jamâl-al-Din visited Shiraz regularly until it became dangerous for him. Jamâlzâde tells the story:

> Although the months of Moharram and Safar were not yet over, one day news arrived that my father was fleeing Shiraz and would soon arrive in Isfahan. Qavâm [explained below] had evidently commissioned a wicked black maid-servant, who was famous in Shiraz for dressing in men's clothes and appearing to be a *luti* (hired thug), to do some injury to my father. One night, thinking it was my father returning home on his donkey, she had struck Seyyed Anayatollâh, one of the city's *rowzeh-khân*s, such a severe blow with a broadsword that the poor man's forehead had been split, and that was why my father came galloping back to Isfahan with some bags of quince and pear seeds called *anchuchak*, which are souvenirs of Shiraz.[22]

Fearing Qavâm, the head of a wealthy and influential family in Shiraz, Seyyed-Jamâl-al-Din decided not to go to Shiraz anymore and instead journeyed to Tabriz. Here Prince Mohammad-'Ali Mirzâ received him warmly and granted him the honorific title of Sadr-al-Mohaqqeqin ('Chief among Scholars'). After this journey to Tabriz, he made a trip to Tehran. As he was about to return to Isfahan, he heard of a *fatwa* to murder Bâbis, issued by Mir Seyyed Hoseyn, the Friday Prayer of Isfahan, and Âqâ Najafi. Jamâlzâde says that his family were certain that if his father set foot in Isfahan, he would disappear, because of his father's association with Mirzâ Asadollâh Khân, "a well-known Bâbî." Jamâlzâde describes the concerns of the family in his memoir:

> Now given the circumstances mentioned earlier, you'll have to admit that my mother had a right to be disturbed and distressed about my father's coming to Isfahan at a time when the goods and property of that city's wretched creatures were at the mercy of a band of rabble and riffraff with turbans on their heads and when the price of a man's life was less than a dog's, the more so when we took omens by opening a volume of Hāfez and this couplet came up:
>
>> We have tested our luck in this city;
>> Our baggage must be drawn out of this abyss.
>
> Without delay, we telegraphed my maternal uncle . . . to inform my father to postpone coming to Isfahan.[23]

Seyyed Jamâl-al-Din's and his friends' ideas of reform provoked conservative clerics who accused them of blasphemy (*kofr*), and later of Bâbism. There are no direct allusions to the Bâbi movement in *The True Dream* but its parody of the high clerical class and critique of the exclusive power of the clergy and Zell-al-Soltân were sufficient for its authors to be accused of sympathies for Bâbism. That accusation could have grave consequences in this period, when Bâbis were both executed by the state and killed in pogroms. Mohammad-'Ali Jamâlzâde recounts in his memoirs several horrifying anecdotes about the execution and 'Bâbi-killings' in this period. He tells how, as a young boy, he witnessed the burning of two merchants who were accused of Bâbi sympathies.[24] Among the alleged Bâbis he met were Sheykh Mohammad Monshâdi of Yazd, an eloquent orator with fresh ideas, who was accused of heresy and forced to leave Tehran. He came to Isfahan where he met Seyyed Jamâl-al-Din and Malek-al-Motakallemin. Another figure was Mirzâ Âqâ Khân Kermâni who visited Isfahan and met Seyyed-Jamâl-al-Din.

It should not be supposed that everyone who was accused of Bâbi sympathies was a Bâbi, or even interested in religion. As Moojen Momen and Mangol Bayat have demonstrated in various detailed studies, there were Bâbis, Azalis and Bâhais among the elite in Iran, but the label was also used for progressive intellectuals and unorthodox religious thinkers.[25] This was so common that anyone who did not participate in the persecution of the 'Bâbis' (most of whom were Bâhais by that time) was likely to be labelled as a Bâbi.

In 1902, Seyyed Jamâl-al-Din moved with his family to Tehran where he started preaching in the Shah mosque. Seyyed Jamâl-al-Din's family's situation grew worse when Mohammad-'Ali Shah (1872–1925) came to power in 1907. Adhering to an anti-constitutionalist policy, and supported by the Russians, he bombarded the Parliament on 23 June 1908. Shortly after, several followers of the constitutional cause were either arrested, exiled or executed. Many of these intellectuals formed the circle of Seyyed-Jamâl-al-Din. Among the prominent persons who were executed, we can name Malek-al-Motakallemin and Mirzâ Jahângir Khan, the editor of *Sur-e Esrâfil*.[26] Seyyed Jamâl-al-Din was an eloquent preacher who knew how to convey new ideas of reform in simple language in his attractive Isfahani tongue. His lectures were well attended. He was also supported by many reform-minded people, including Seyyed Mohammad Tabâtabâ'i and Seyyed 'Abdollâh Behbahâni. In 1905 the leader of Friday prayers in Tehran, Hâjj Seyyed Abu'l-Qâsem, cunningly insisted that he should give a lecture. Seyyed Jamâl-al-Din accepted and from the pulpit of the Shah Mosque, he criticized the governor of Tehran, 'Alâ'-al-Dowle, saying, "if the king is a Muslim, he should support the 'ulamâ, listening to their fair advice, otherwise."[27] At this moment, the Friday prayer leader started to shout, "unbeliever (*bi-din*), apostate (*lâ madhhab*), why are you disrespecting the king of Muslims?" and, "bring this Bâbi down!" A fight began between the supporters of the Constitutional government and its opponents, the supporters of Mohammad-'Ali Shah. Seyyed Jamâl-al-Din fled the mosque and hid in the house of Seyyed Mohammad Tabâtabâ'i, and for one night in the house of Mirzâ Yahyâ Dowlatâbâdi, "a secret Azali and a prominent leader in the movement to introduce modern education."[28] The supporters of the constitution, together with Seyyed Jamâl-al-Din, began a sit-in protest in the Parliament, which lasted several weeks, until Mohammad-'Ali Shah with Russian support bombarded the Parliament. Many of the constitutionalists were imprisoned and executed. Seyyed Jamâl-al-Din hid in the house of one of his friends. Later he went to Hamadân where he stayed for several weeks. He wanted to go to his uncle in Najaf but his story reached the governor of Hamadân, Mozaffar-al-Molk, who initially treated Seyyed Jamâl-al-Din respectfully but secretly informed Mohammad-'Ali Shah. Soon he received a telegram from Mohammad-'Ali Shah to hand Seyyed-Jamâl-al-Din over to the governor of Borujerd and Lorestân, Amir Afkham Qarâgozlu. He imprisoned Seyyed Jamâl-al-Din for several months until he was strangled in his cell, at the orders of Mohammad-'Ali Shah, in 1908 (1326 qamari). Choubiné writes that Seyyed Jamâl-al-Din's mausoleum is in the vicinity of Borujerd and that people were still visiting his grave.[29]

A sermon by Seyyed Jamâl-al-Din

Seyyed Jamâl-al-Din's sermons were published in the journal *al-Jamâl*, by Mirzâ Mohammad-Hoseyn Esfahâni in Tehran, containing the sermons and writings of Seyyed Jamâl-al-Din.[30] As referred to previously, his sermons were so popular that they also drew the attention of Europeans living in Tehran. Edouard Valmont's journal of the events during the Constitutional Revolution was published by Eustache de Lorey and Douglas Sladen. Valmont devotes an entire chapter to one of the sermons of Seyyed Jamâl-al-Din, which is cited here in its entirety for its merits and significance.[31] In the preface to the book, in which Douglas Sladen comments on its "fascinating subject," he singles out Seyyed Jamâl-al-Din's sermon as an "extraordinary account of a political sermon preached by the mulla whom Valmont calls Seyyed Jamal-ud-Din, which shows more than anything else in the book, the trend of thought and spread of education among the Persian Constitutionalists." He then concludes, "This struck me as more interesting than anything that I had read about the Bâbi movement in Persia."[32]

The sermon is indeed fascinating for several reasons. To begin with, it gives us insight into the type of subjects these progressive clergy preached and how they structured their sermons rhetorically, stirring the audience to a certain direction. In this sermon, Seyyed Jamâl-al-Din talks about Equality, Security, Liberty and Art and Science, trying to reconcile these subjects with Islamic law and the Koran. When he talks about equality, he courageously says that all subjects of the nation are equal before the law, whether one is the Shah, a prince or a beggar. In talking about these subjects, Seyyed Jamâl-al-Din relates these subtly to the fruits of the European political system, which has offered Europe such technological progress. He is so impressed by the degree of European scientific progress that he gives several examples, putting them in a rhetorically rich frame when he talks to people. For instance, on the science of telegraphy he says,

> Thou speakest, and thy words go forth and are recorded in London, without the intervention of either wire or pole! Yet is it not a bird that serves thee

as messenger, neither is it the wind that carries thy saying! O men, O men, whence cometh all this? Know ye, indeed? Then will I tell it you! This is the fruit of science! Of science! Of science! And indeed science! science existeth not in Persia!

Afterwards, he continues to astound his audience with an example from the field of medicine:

They have invented an instrument whereby the unborn child may be seen in the womb of the mother: whereby, if she be ill, the seat of the mischief may be discovered, the secret of the wound revealed. With this instrument can men behold that which is contained within a box the cover whereof is securely padlocked. And all this cometh by science only – by God, I swear it – science! It is not magic, it is not delusion, it is not miracle.

The sermon is rhetorically rich, poetically strong and organizationally clever. The way Seyyed Jamâl-al-Din structures his sermons around his subject, using improvisations, poetry, parables and metaphors, is mesmerizing. The parables and metaphors he uses to create parallels with the political situation of the time are superb. The journal gives extraordinarily vivid descriptions of the way his crowded audience reacted. Seyyed Jamâl-al-Din talks about delicate and daring subjects for an audience who hang on his every word:

"AL-HAMDULLAH!" cried Mirzâ Jafar, "you will at last be able to hear a sermon from the sublime! Agha Sayyid Jamal-ud-Din!"
And he proceeded to explain that this celebrated preacher, at the urgent request of his followers, whose numbers far overflowed his accustomed mosque, would address them that afternoon on the Sabz-i-Maydan, and it would be quite possible for us to form part of his audience without, at the same time, coming in contact with the crowd, which might very possibly resent the intrusion of an Infidel. His friend, the tobacconist, was willing to admit us to the roof of his bazar, and from thence we should be able to hear everything perfectly.
I was extremely gratified by this news: to hear a sermon by a mujtahid, one of the heads of the Persian clergy, a descendant of the Prophet himself, was a unique privilege, and the more so in this case since this particular holy personage was, according to his own expression, "the first Mussulman preacher who had preached Liberty to the congregation of the Faithful."
We lost no time in setting out for the Sabz-i-Maydan – The Green Square – reaching the Tobacco Bazar by a circuitous route to avoid the crowd, and the worthy merchant led us up on to the terrace, where the company, although considerable, was select and sufficiently well-educated to conceal any resentment they might feel at the presence of a Frank like myself.
Below us the maydan literally swarmed with the Faithful; *kula*s of astrachan jostled *kula*s of khaki felt, with here and there a fleck of colour, white or

blue or green, marking out the wearer of a turban, whilst on the edges of the crowd the groups of women formed a sombre outline.

In front of the beautiful pointed doorway which, like a triumphal arch, forms the entrance to the bazar, was placed a pulpit, a wooden arm-chair raised on three or four steps.

All at once the crowd parted, and disclosed the figure of the Sayyid, whom I recognised from the glimpse I had had of him in the Booksellers' Bazar. He walked slowly, with dignity, and yet with humility, of the exaggerated type affected by the higher Persian clergy. An ample black *aba* hung from his shoulders to the ground, and his ascetic features were surmounted by an enormous dark blue turban. He was received by all with profound salutations, and some even drew near to kiss his hands or the skirts of his robe.

He mounted the pulpit amidst a murmur of respectful approbation, and lifting his head towards heaven, his hands raised, palms upwards, to the height of his shoulders, he began the invocation:

"Bismillah er-Rahman, er-Rahim, Rabb-al-Alamin!" (In the Name of God, the Clement, the Merciful, Master of the Worlds!)

Then he gazed around him, smiling, passed his delicate hand over his face, and spoke in these words, which, thanks to the assistance of Mirzâ Jafar, I have been able faithfully to transcribe: –

"I have said to you, O men, that the principle of progress and of prosperity, of wealth and of power, of well-being in this world and of salvation in the next, dependeth upon four essentials. Every country, every nation that possesseth these four essentials advanceth along the way of progress, and riseth from the obscure deeps of profound darkness to the loftiest and most resplendent heights of light. Every nation, on the other hand, in which these four essentials may not be found, every country which lacketh be it but one of them, possessing indeed the other three, endureth a condition of ruin and desolation such as we behold around us in Persia at this moment. Its people are in poverty, in weakness, and in ignorance. It is the lack of these four essentials that rendereth man ignorant and incapable, it is this that conduceth to his poverty and wretchedness, and in this state it is that he seeketh no more after anything, neither laboureth any more with his hands, nor hath in his heart any desire but that he may be annihilated.

"Know ye, O men, these are the four essentials:

"(1) Equality; (2) Security; (3) Liberty; (4) Art and Science.

"Last night I said unto you that this word 'Equality' doth not pretend that, for example, I am to sit side by side with the Shah, the Protector of Islam; it doth not pretend that the soldier is to be equipped as the general; it doth not pretend that ye shall no longer respect nor kiss the hands of ulamas. To believe thus would be to err profoundly. And similarly with the word 'Liberty,' which some would turn from its primary meaning, and which I will, if it please Allah, explain unto you in its proper sequence.

"But this is the meaning of the word 'Equality': the laws of God shall be applied in an equal manner to every unit of the nation, that is to say, whosoever stealeth shall lose his hand; whosoever partaketh of wine shall receive chastisement; whosoever hath property liable to tribute shall pay the tribute levied thereon!"

Here Mirzâ Jafar murmured in my ear, "It costs him nothing to say that, because the property of priests is exempt from taxation!"

"Whosoever it may be," went on the Sayyid, "without excuse or exception, for in the Koran and in the Hadith is no difference made between the Shah and the beggar. The Koran saith, 'Be exact in fulfilling your prayers!' This command is addressed to all, and concerns each one of us. No man can say, 'I am a Sayyid, and therefore I am exempt from prayer!' Or again 'I am a witness in Islam,' or 'I am a prince!' Prayer bindeth on all, save only such as are explicitly exempted by the Law, as, for example, a woman at the period of her menstruation. Whosoever a woman may be, if she prostitute herself, she shall fall into hell-fire, unless it be that she repenteth. Therefore see we that 'Equality' intendeth 'The Ordinance of God is the same for all men.'

"O Men! The God Who should make distinctions between His creatures would not be God; the Law that included not all beneath its rule, both high and low, would not be law! God hath said, 'O Men, fasting is ordained for you!' and thenceforth each one, no matter who he be, is bound to fast – man or woman, young or old, rich or poor, with the exception of such as are exempt, as the sick, or he who maketh a journey. What difference can there be between thee when ill and me when ill? And thus it is also with obligatory almsgiving, with pilgrimages, with the Holy War: this, then, is the meaning of the word 'Equality.'

"Here in our land of Persia this law holdeth not to-day. I say not that it hath lapsed for this year only; it holdeth not in this present year, for that it held not in the year before this, neither did it so ten years previously, or even a hundred years. And herein is the reason wherefore we grow daily poorer and poorer, and become each day more and more miserable, more and more wretched!"

Here Agha Sayyid Jamal-ud-Din paused, and murmurs of "Barik-Allah!" "Mash-Allah!" ("Praise to Allah!") came from all round; a movement as of a billow swept over the vast assembly, little groups of critics gathered here and there, commenting on the words of the Descendant of the Prophet, all applauding his utterances, and delighting in the vistas opened up by them to their fertile Eastern imaginations.

The Sayyid had assumed his aerial chair, and was slowly stroking the end of his beard, tinted with henna and rang; his small, piercing eyes shone in their deep sockets like stars reflected at the bottom of a well; a frozen smile curled, somewhat sardonically, his sensual mouth, which a moustache, cut straight above the lips, shadowed with a black line, drooping at the corners. And behind him the blue faience of the portal shone in the sunlight like an aureole.

He continued:

"Philosophers and scholars have drawn their wisdom from the prophets; all that we have, therefore, comes to us from the prophets. Neither have these invented anything of themselves, all that they have taught us they have obtained from God.

"Our feeble intellect can determine nothing by its own calculations!"

And he pointed his phrase by that argument so supreme to the Persian mind, a quotation from the poets:–

> It but admits what Science first hath shown;
> All Art, be sure, is Inspiration-born,
> For this comes first – with Intellect as crown.

"Astronomy, medicine, these are gifts brought to us through the revelations of the prophets. Of what use is intellect, of what use feeling in that which is without form?

> It needs but little wit to dig a grave,
> With this what part can Thought or Science have?

"Had God not said, 'Bury ye your dead!' we should not have known what we were to do with them, even as Cabil (Cain), who for long knew not what he should do with the body of Abil (Abel). God it was Who instructed him in the rites of burial. Had the prophets not said, 'Wash ye your linen!' we should not have known the necessity for so doing. In short, all our knowledge cometh from the prophets, who received it themselves of God.

"'Neither doth he speaks of his own will. It is no other than a revelation which hath been revealed unto him.'

"God speaketh in allegories; that is to say, when He would bring to our intelligence that which hath been hidden therefrom, He revealeth it unto us after the manner of a parable, so that both I and thou may understand. If, for example, He desireth us to understand the perishable nature of this present world, He embodieth His thought in metaphor, comparing the world unto a spider's web. As thus: 'But the weakest of all houses is the house of the spider,' by which we must understand that this world is as fragile as a spider's web.

"His Highness Jesus, in the Gospels, hath made great use of apologues, as hath Moses in his books, and again, God, in the Koran. 'Moreover, God will not be ashamed to propound in a parable a gnat.'

"I speak openly that all may understand.

"Neither is this an evil work, seeing that it is the work of the Prophet. When one has to do with children, one must speak the language of childhood.

"God Himself is the first to employ the allegory as a channel for knowledge, and to elaborate this point would carry us too far. Doth He not say, for instance:

"'Verily, the idols which ye invoke beside God can never create a single fly, although they were all assembled for that purpose; and if the fly snatch anything from them, they cannot recover the same from it'?

"God here desireth to show us that idolatry is evil, and it is by this parable that He thus instructeth us. In the second half of this verse we have an allusion to the custom of the ancient idolaters of that time of anointing their idols with must [unfermented wine], this must being subsequently collected in vessels and used for affections of the throat and other maladies, upon which must the flies were wont to settle.

"It is said that a certain Arab, possessing an idol, went forth one day upon his business. On his return he beheld a fox defiling this idol. Then cried he aloud and said, 'Is this a God to be worshipped, whose head can thus be defiled by foxes?'

"And this is an example which may yet serve in our day, which may serve, above all, for those – and I ask pardon of God for that which I am about to say – for those who abandon the religion of the Amir of the Faithful, His Highness Ali, and become Bâbis; Allah Akbar! Forgive me! These are so far demented as to imagine that a man can become God. By my most holy ancestor the Prophet, these men are worse than the ungodly in the days of ignorance! Go to, do ye imagine that mere flesh and blood, born of woman as are we, suffering hunger, weariness, the need of clothing, as do we, subject to maladies, obliged to submit like any other to the ministrations of the apothecary, do ye think, I say, that such an one can become God?"

There were shouts of "No! no!" and "Blasphemy" from the crowd. Mirzâ Jafar, beside me, grew pale. In this great concourse of people there were, doubtless, as I knew, a considerable number of Bâbis – there are said to be some thirty thousand in Teheran – and I suspected myself that these indignant protestations came chiefly from them, for since the cruel persecutions to which they have been subjected they hide their real religious convictions, like the Sufis of old, behind a skilful *katman*.

"In short," continued Jamal-ud-Din, "these parables which we have in the Koran, and which have been much added to by the philosophers, have all been written in the ways of wisdom. Grave doctrines have been clothed in the garments of fable, so that all may imbibe them with pleasure. The earliest writers of allegory among men were the philosophers of India.

"Three gifts have we received from India. The first is the game of chess, whereby men learn to conquer kingdoms by means of strategy, and which is, on this account, of the greatest value to kings. It accustometh a man to consider well his moves, and whereby he may best achieve those which shall ultimately follow. But this game, in the eyes of our religious law, is forbidden.

"The second gift is the science of mathematics. The Indians it was who invented the nine numerical symbols whereby we are enabled to inscribe millions of numbers, the addition of a zero sufficing to mark enormous differences in value.

"The third gift is that of the story-books, books, that is to say, wherein the problems of wisdom are clad in the garments of anecdote, so that even children, even women read them with eagerness. The best of these story-books is that of Kalila and Dimnah, the translation whereof is Anvari

Sohaili, a work of such great excellence that it hath been given in all the tongues of the world. We owe the Persian version to King Anuchirvan, who at great expense imported the book from India and caused it to be translated into our tongue.

"After the Indian philosophers, we find that the Franks, with their usual perfection of attainment, have produced many excellent books of this nature, called by them 'Novels,' books of such profound usefulness that I say unto you, take ye them and read them, O ye who have understanding of the Frankish tongues!

"Verily, I know not yet whether the peoples of Europe have attained any greater heights of civilization than this.

"We imagined that in telegraphy science had reached its highest level. Here in Teheran a man moves his hand and lo, the sound thereof re-echoes in Paris. Yet learned we ere long that there was a wonder greater than this, even the telephone. Thou speakest here, and thy voice, thy voice, thy own voice is heard at Kasvin. Nor was the end yet, for we behold a still greater marvel, the wireless telegraphy. Thou speakest, and thy words go forth and are recorded in London, without the intervention of either wire or pole! Yet is it not a bird that serves thee as messenger, neither is it the wind that carries thy saying! O men, O men, whence cometh all this? Know ye, indeed? Then will I tell it you! This is the fruit of science! Of science! Of science! And indeed science! science existeth not in Persia!

"Ya Ali! Amán! Amán!" ("O Ali Mercy! Mercy!") cried some of his hearers, and the Descendant of the Prophet, having gulped down a few mouthfuls of water from an earthen bowl held up to him by a water carrier, went on, amidst the silence and deep attention of the astonished faithful:

"Ah, yes! We have, on the other hand, a science amongst us which hath made strange progress in our midst, it is the science of 'blackguardism and theft'! To-night thou returnest home in peace unto thine house, thou slumberest, and to-morrow thou art ejected therefrom, for that a man hath forged unto himself proprietary titles and thine house hath been sold unto another! How many such thieves are there not in Teheran! And to what pains do they not go to acquire knowledge, to learn and to apply all the tricks of their trade of robbery!

"The men of the Franks have brought all things unto their proper point of perfection; for instance, medicine. They have invented an instrument whereby the unborn child may be seen in the womb of the mother: whereby, if she be ill, the seat of the mischief may be discovered, the secret of the wound revealed. With this instrument can men behold that which is contained within a box the cover whereof is securely padlocked. And all this cometh by science only – by God, I swear it – science! It is not magic, it is not delusion, it is not miracle.

"Moreover, this same science hath attained unto great heights also in the realm of political economy, and in social questions and matters of government. How often have I not told you that a country which hath two thousand millions of taxes sees to their payment through its subjects themselves, and should a collector desire to appropriate one single *toman* of all these mighty sums, it would immediately be discovered, and that because of the height whereunto science hath been brought by the Franks."

"Ajab! Astonishment! Marvel!" cried the crowd, finger on lip, in token of admiration. But the preacher, with a brusque movement, as if to check these sentiments towards Europe, went on at once:

"And now that we have a deliberative national Majlis, this is not in order that we may adopt the laws of Infidels, *Al-Hamdullah*! *we have the best laws in the world, since to us belongeth the Koran*! But what we must borrow from the Franks is their mode of nominating officials, the regulations as to Ministers, their method of levying taxes in such wise that none shall be subjected to violence."

At this moment there was a considerable stir among the crowd at the other side of the maydan; two men of the regiment of the Amir Bahadur Jang, easily recognizable by their attire, coming out of a tea-house, began yelling out "*Padar Mashruta misuzanim*!" ("We burn the father of the Constitution!") A space cleared before them, as if by magic, the women uttering shrill cries. Their well-known brutality, the long poignards hanging from their belts, and the guns slung over their shoulders, butt-end upwards, inspired a well-merited fear. A few "Bull-Necks" were on the point of attacking them, but a mulla restrained them, fortunately, for Allah alone knows what would have happened had they come to blows. The presence of the Sayyid in the pulpit served to overawe these brutes of soldiers, who left the maydan immediately.

But the incident, rousing as it did the spirit of political hatred, had disturbed the audience. There were angry exclamations on every side. The sun had disappeared behind a dark cloud, the cold became biting.

But Jamal-ud-Din remained unmoved. In a flash he had once more gripped his audience, who, shivering with cold as they were, became again all attention. His voice sounded more ringing, more sonorous than ever, there was in it a note of anger.

"O people of Teheran!" he said, "thank God a thousand thousand times that ye dwell in the capital! The Prophet saith, 'Dwell in populous places, that if one man oppress you ye may carry your complaint unto another.'

"I have sworn by Allah, I swear also by the Imam of Time, I swear it by the holy Koran, I swear it by the Lord of the Confessors of Islam, the matter of the Majlis was a work beyond the power of all, and it is the Imam Mahdi who hath accomplished it, by awakening you from the slumber of indifference that I might speak to you as I do from the lofty place of this pulpit!

"O people of Teheran, I have no desire, be assured, to flatter any man, but the development, the progress of this deliberate Majlis are due, under the Master of Time, to the efforts of two great Sayyids – both Witnesses and Proofs of Islam; I mean, Agha Sayyid Mohammed Mujtahid, and Agha Sayyid Abdullah, who have continually cried unto you, 'O men, tyranny is abroad on the earth, set up, therefore, a *Majlis* of Justice!'

"May Allah advance every mulla who hath come to your assistance, nor thought of himself, nor sought to plunder you that he might live in luxury upon your ruins!

"O men, if it come to your ears that certain traitors, certain wicked ones desire to go against this *Majlis*, have ye no fear! It will be as I have already told unto you so often! These men are lower than the mosquitoes, less are they than the mosquitoes of the mosquitoes! Say ye unto them: 'We must bring prosperity unto our country, we must carry out the commands of God, we must give riches unto you, we desire that there should no longer be so many beggars, men or women, in want and misery by day and night in our streets!'"

"Hear ye a parable! One day the mosquitoes came before His Highness Sulayman (King Solomon) to complain unto him; and thus said they: 'O prophet of God, what can we do against the wind which torments and tortures us? If four of us but meet together, behold the wind is there also scattereth us!" And Solomon called,

> 'O Winds, come hither!'
> The wind heard his call, came up with violent raging, strenuous and impetuous,
> Whereupon the mosquito straightway took flight.
> Then cried Solomon unto him: 'Whither goest thou, O mosquito?
> Remain, that I may pronounce judgement between you.'
> But the mosquito answered him, 'O King my death comes, from his life,
> And his breath obscures the mirror of my days.
> When he appears, how shall I resist him?
> Alas, he torments me, and does me to death!'[33]

"Behold, these froward ones are like unto the mosquitoes!

"O men, know ye not the *Majlis* shall bring forth from his tomb the father of the bribes; it shall burn the father of the gaming-houses; none shall have the right any more to issue commands against justice, nor any be henceforth permitted to gather up bank-notes by night that he may bring disturbance unto the city in the morning. *Al-Hamdullah*! We are the Servants of the Law. *Al-Hamdullah*! We are the Servants of Persia. We will unite in our efforts to bring prosperity unto Persia, to guard her from falling into the hands of her enemies. The Shah, the Protector of Islam, is in perfect harmony with the *Majlis*, and more than another he knoweth the fruit and the *kibla* (aim) of this institution. Beware, therefore, lest ye cause him annoyance, and when the *Majlis* shall be firmly established, then will the mosquito go of his own accord!"

Seyyed Mirzâ Nasrollâh Beheshti (Malek-al-Motakallemin)

Malek-al-Motakallemin was born in Isfahan in 1864, and studied a traditional curriculum and the history of religions and philosophy in Isfahan to the age of twenty-three.³⁴ He then went on pilgrimage to Mecca, followed by a visit to the holy shrines in Iraq. Afterwards he journeyed to India where he stayed two years, visiting various cities including Calcutta and Bombay. In India he wrote a book, *Men al-Khalq ela al-haqq* (*From People to the Truth*), which he published with the assistance of the Parsees in India. This treatise attacks the Shiite clergy, criticizing several of their practices. The Isma'ili Shiites and their leader, the Âqâ Khân, considered the criticism to be an insult to Shiism and to God, accusing Malek-al-Motakallemin of heresy. Malek-al-Motakallemin returned to Iran through the Persian Gulf harbour city of Bushehr. To earn a living, he travelled to the towns around Isfahan, especially in the months of Moharram and Safar. He even journeyed to Tabriz where he stayed for two years. Prince Mozaffar-al-Din Mirzâ, who had heard his preaching, treated him respectfully, giving him a robe of honour and the honorific title Malek-al-Motakallemin.

When he wished to return to Isfahan he was concerned about the anti-Bâbi sentiments there (directed in fact at the Bâha'is and Azalis). He too was accused of being a Bâbi. He contacted the governor of Isfahan, Zell-al-Soltân, who assured him he would be safe and invited him to return. After a period of silence and thoughtful preaching, Malek-al-Motakallemin started to criticize conservative clerics and the government. Âqâ Najafi declared him a corrupt person. Malek-al-Motakallemin had to leave Isfahan. He went to Tehran, where the reformist Minister Amin-al-Dowle and the influential ayatollah Seyyed Mohammad Tabâtabâ'i supported him, even allowing him to preach at his own mosque.³⁵ Through the mediation of Amin-al-Dowle, he became a teacher at the Roshdiyye school, which taught a modern curriculum. He came into contact with Sheykh Hâdi Najm-Âbâdi whose unorthodox ideas influenced him. After a while he went to Gilân and spent some time in Rasht where he preached, including a critique of the clerics. Soon Hojjat-al-Eslâm Khomâmi declared him a heretic.

Malek-al-Motakallemin then went to the Caspian harbour city of Anzali, and then, via Baku (Bâdkube) and Asjchabad (Ishqâbâd), he headed for Mashhad. Here he stayed several nights at Gowharshâd Mosque where he also preached to earn some money to go to Tehran. From Tehran he went to Isfahan to visit his family. Afterwards he went to Shiraz where he started to give lectures, criticizing the clergy and the government. The governor of Shiraz exiled him to Isfahan but, because of Âqâ Najafi's fatwa against him, he could not enter Isfahan and stayed in a town near Isfahan. He continued fighting for freedom and constitutional government, directing his condemnation at Mohammad-'Ali Shah. After the bombardment of the parliament in 1908, he was hanged in the Bâgh-e Shah together with his friend Mirzâ Jahângir Khan, the editor of *Sur-e Esrâfil*.³⁶

Ahmad Kasravi gives a report of his death, on the basis of an eye witness, Mirzâ 'Ali-Akbar Khân Ardâqi, who was in chains in the Bâgh-e Shah with others:

> The severe hardships of Wednesday night eventually came to an end. We woke up in the morning to see that the Cossacks had fettered eight persons on one chain and were taking them out. After transporting eight persons, they would transport another group of eight. My brother and Hâjji

Malek-al-Motakallemin used to eat opium. Opium was brought to them. After a while, two guards came to take Malek and Mirzâ Jahângir. They removed them from the chained group of eight and put chains on their hands, shouting: "Rise! Come!" It was as if both of them knew that they wanted to take them to their deaths. At the door, Malek sang loudly and melodiously the following poem:

> We attended one audience, and this oppression was brought upon us;
> What would be done to those who live at the enemy's court?

He sang this and turned to go out the door. We were all stricken with sorrow. This sorrow multiplied when we saw the two guards coming back with the chains they had put on the necks of Malek and Mirzâ Jahângir Khân. They threw the chains into the room and we were certain that the lives of those two poor men had come to an end.[37]

Ahmad Kasravi refers several times to the preaching of Seyyed Jamâl-al-Din and Malek-al-Motakallemin and how they wanted to spread the message of liberalism, underestimating the power of the Shah:

> afterward, the associations (*anjoman*s) would come together every day in the Sepahsâlâr school and Seyyed Jamâl-al-Din and Malek-al-Motakallemin would speak while expressing ill-words about the court and the king. They would send messages to him on behalf of the Iranian nation. They did all these things but the thought did not occur to them that they also needed support. You would say that they did not understand that if the Shah wanted, he would disperse them by the force of weapons and uproot the Parliament. They would not believe such a thing. On this point one must say that they were very inexperienced.[38]

Kasravi is equally critical to others as well when he says: "It is more remarkable that neither the parliament nor these associations would send messages to the towns, asking their support. Indeed, they were so naïve that they did not find it necessary, thinking that their own excitement, activities and commotion were enough to withstand the court."[39] Kasravi's appraisal of the situation points at a lack of coordination between ordinary people and the intellectuals, whether religious or secular.

In the history of Iranian Constitutional movement, Malek-al-Motakallemin is known for his role as the head of the Revolutionary Committee, which consisted of fifty-seven "radical intellectuals."[40]

Hâjj Mirzâ Ahmad Kermâni (Majd al-Eslâm)

Hâjj Mirzâ Ahmad was a friend of Malek-al-Motakallemin and Seyyed Jamâl-al-Din, frequenting secret meetings in Isfahan. In *The History of Iranian Men*

(*Târikh-e rajâl-e Irân*), Hâjj Mirzâ Ahmad is described as a learned man with an excellent memory and fine calligraphic skills. When it was discovered that he was a Bâbi, Mortazâ-Qoli Khân Wakil-al-Molk bastinadoed him. As they beat him with a stick, Hâjj Mirzâ Ahmad started to recite verses from the Koran. They continued to beat him and no one mediated to stop this. He looked at the men who were beating him and said, "don't you think it's enough?" Wakil-al-Molk had to laugh at this and ordered them to stop. He exiled him to Neyriz. Hâjj Mirzâ Ahmad stayed there for a while but later he went to Rayy, near Tehran, and stayed at the school in the complex of Hazrat ʿAbd-al-ʿAzim.

He was arrested in Tehran on 25 April 1891, together with a number of other people. In his memoir, Hâjj Mohammad-ʿAli Mahallâti, known as Sayyâh (1836–1925), refers several times to Hâjj Mirzâ Ahmad and his imprisonment. At one point he mentions that when Kâmrân Mirzâ was hunting for Bâbis, he also sought to accuse and arrest Hâjji Sayyâh, Hâjj Mirzâ Ahmad and a number of others. Hâjj Sayyâh depicts the situation of the prisoners in several pages of his memoir. Of Hâjj Mirzâ Ahmad, he writes,

> when Hâjj Mirzâ Ahmad was in prison in Qazvin, his wife died. His two sons, one of them six years old, approached Amin-al-Soltân, saying, "We do not have a house or shelter!" Amin-al-Soltân sent them to Qazvin. The older son received a job in the *âbdâr-khâne* of Saʾd-al-Saltane but the other son stayed in prison with his father.[41]

Choubiné adds that Browne's report, based as it is on Mohammad Qazvini's explication, is not clear enough, because Mirzâ Rezâ Kermâni (the assassin of Nâser-al-Din Shah) stayed with Hâjj Mirzâ Ahmad when he was seeking to find the right moment to kill the Shah. Choubiné continues that during Mirzâ Rezâ Kermâni's interrogation, when he was asked about his contacts, he said that he was in contact with Hâjj Mirzâ Ahmad and a Seyyed, whom he did not know. Both were ready to go on a journey.[42] When he was asked whether they were heading to Hamadân, Kermâni answered, "By God, I do not know which direction they took. I only know that they opened the Koran (*estekhare*) to see which direction they should go. Their bibliomancy showed a good omen to go to the upper road to Kahrizak and they started their journey."

Choubiné surmises that Hâjj Mirzâ Ahmad and the Seyyed learned of Mirzâ Rezâ Kermâni's assassination plans and tried to be away from Tehran. Immediately after the assassination, two people are arrested in Hamadân, Hâjj Mirzâ Ahmad and Seyyed Hasan Sâheb-Zamâni, who may be the Seyyed mentioned previously.[43] Initially the assassination was attributed to the Bâbis and a hunt to arrest and execute Bâbis began. Later, the government discovered that the plan to murder the Shah was hatched by followers of Seyyed Jamâl al-Din Asadâbâdi (Afghâni).[44] While Hâjj Mirzâ Ahmad died in prison of dysentery, Seyyed Hasan Sâheb-Zamâni was released after a period, when Moshir-al-Saltane, his uncle, pleaded for him. Seyyed Hasan went to Mashhad where he remained for the rest of his life.

The plot of *The True Dream*

In this treatise, the authors describe a dream of the Day of Resurrection, when all the leading clerical and political men of Isfahan are called by the Lord and asked to justify their actions, such as wasting public money, oppression and embezzlement. Bahrâm Choubiné states that the setting reminds the reader of Persian ascension stories, in which an individual journeys through several spheres until the climax of the story, when they encounter the Creator, similar to Dante's *Divina Comedia*. However, *The True Dream* does not recount a journey; rather, it concentrates on the encounter with God on the Day of Judgement, when the dead come to life and are expected to answer God's questions about their actions in this world. The choice of the setting is brilliant, as it offers the authors, themselves members of the respected clerical class, the opportunity to judge their opponents from God's perspective. The voice of God, speaking offstage, condemns the behaviour of the clerics and their deviant interpretations of the Koran and Islamic traditions, and sends them to punishment. Often a flabbergasted God cannot believe how the senior clerics have failed to apply His words, or have interpreted Him to suit their own economic, social or political purposes. The clerics' responses to God are in many cases comical.

In the second half of the nineteenth century, several treatises and books were written to introduce European political philosophy or to critique the Persian way of life and socio-political situation. *The True Dream* certainly bears comparison to Âkhundzâde's *Maktubât*, Mirzâ Âqâ Khân Kermâni's *Sad Khetâbe*, Talebov's *Masâlek al-Mohsenin*, Mostashâr al-Dowle's *Yek Kalame*, Zeyn-al-'Âbedin Marâghe'i's *Siyâhat-nâme Ebrâhim Beg* and several other valuable works.[45] Together, these works played an enormous role in the 'awakening' of the Iranian people. As Bahram Choubiné rightly states, the difference between *The True Dream* and other comparable books is that this book was written by three authors living within Iran and that it names its targets, those who oppress the people, depicting their actions, asking them questions and forcing them to answer in the court of God.[46] When the book was distributed in Iran, its authors remained anonymous, which led to confusion for some time, which Choubiné has described. The book has also been confused with other books with similar titles, such as *Kh^{w}âb-e khalse*, which is better known as *Kh^{w}âb-nâme* (*Record of a Dream*), written by Mohammad-Hasan Khan E'temâd al-Saltane.[47] Several books of the period couch their narrative as a dream or something experienced between wakefulness and sleep. Elsewhere I have referred to such treatises and why awakening, sleeping and even the lullaby became notable metaphors.[48] For the Persian authors of this period, 'awakening' the people meant to enthuse them to participate in social and political affairs to establish a constitutional government. One treatise that uses a dream allegory to indicate what the author wished to achieve for Iran is *One Word*, by Mostashâr-al-Dowle, who begins by saying:

> One day ... I could not sleep. I thought I saw a messenger from the unseen, standing between heaven and earth, who appeared from the West and faced the lands of Islam. He cried aloud: "O travellers in the path of the Shari'a, the

ruler of mankind, and O you zealous leaders of the people of Islam! *Where is your victory and authority and where is your wealth and knowledge.* Why in this age do you sit, negligent and useless, and why do you pay no attention to the progress made by other peoples? Your neighbors have brought the wilds of the mountains into the circle of civilization[49] while you are still denying the progress of Europe.[50]

The dreamy state is a metaphor for the condition of Iran and would entice the reader to be awakened.[51] A somewhat later work that uses this metaphor is Nâzem-al-Eslâm Kermâni's *Târikh-e Bidâri-ye Irâniyân* (*History of the Awakening of the Iranians*).[52]

History of the text and publications

According to Malekzâde, *The True Dream* was published in Iran in 1318 (1900–1) and created a tumult. Thousands of handwritten copies were made and distributed in various cities in Iran. Malekzâde continues, "afterwards, the book was published in St. Petersburg and in India."[53] Passages from *The True Dream* were also published by Jamâlzâde in his *Sar-o tah yek karbâs* and by Mehdi Malekzâde in his *History of the Iranian Constitutional Revolution*. It was also published as an appendix to E. Yaghmâ'i's *Shahid-e râh-e âzâdi*.[54] Jamâlzâde mentions that the treatise was published several times, including once in Baku. Choubiné's text is based on the version published in number fourteen of the journal *Armaghân* (1312/1933).[55] In this publication, Seyyed Jamâl-al-Din is named as the only author, but in issue five of the journal in the same year, it is reported that an informed man from Isfahan had sent a letter advising the editors that the persons who assisted Seyyed Jamâl-al-Din in writing *The True Dream* were Malek-al-Motakallemin, Hâjj Fâteh al-Molk and Mirzâ Asadollâh Khan, the clerk at the Russian Embassy. This source in Isfahan also writes, "before the book was published, several copies existed in Isfahan and Tehran and were disseminated among people. Zell-al-Soltân seriously desired to find the authors and punish them. Due to the pact that the authors had among themselves, their names were not revealed. Zell-al-Soltân suspected Seyyed Jamâl-al-Din as the author more than others. For this reason, Seyyed Jamâl-al-Din fled to Tehran. Sometime later, the book was published in Russia. Then Zell-al-Soltân ascribed the book to Russians and stopped his hunt for the authors."[56] Choubiné says that his edition might have some defects as it is based on the text published in Armaghân, and the editors of this journal might have intentionally or unintentionally removed passages. He then asks the readers to send him a fuller manuscript so that he can amend the text in later editions. To my knowledge, *The True Dream* has not been published since 1986, the date of Choubiné's publication. This is not surprising, considering the situation in contemporary Iran.

The book's literary merits

The True Dream is one of the new satirical literary books written in the modern era, using colloquial language and even the dialect of Isfahan. It can be considered a forerunner of the popular satirical genre in modern Persian, as its style was adopted by several other literati at the beginning of the twentieth century, especially ʿAli-Akbar Dehkhodâ and Mohammad-ʿAli Jamâlzâde, who imitates *The True Dream* in his *Sahrâ-ye mahshar* (*The Plain of Resurrection*).[57] This is hardly surprising as Jamâlzade was the son of Seyyed Jamâl-al-Din, one of the authors. Seyyed Jamâl-al-Din had an interest in literature in general and modern literature in particular. As we have seen in Seyyed Jamâl-al-Din's sermon, he not only spoke about equality, liberty and freedom but also praised novels as a new genre capable of reaching a broad public. His simple, direct and accessible style of preaching has already been noted. His son Jamâlzâde, who later became a pioneer of modern Persian fiction, also adopted simple language, and a critical portrayal of the clerical class, in his short stories.

One of the merits of *The True Dream*, which makes the work lively and refreshing, is that it is couched in the form of a comic play. During the second half of the nineteenth century, dramas resembling Western plays were introduced to Persia and several plays were written to address a wide range of social and political subjects.[58] *The True Dream* is not the first Persian play. Mirzâ Fath-ʿAli Âkhundzâde (1812–78) was perhaps the first Iranian intellectual who couched his protests against traditional Islamic "values, customs and beliefs" in the form of modern plays, in which he champions the position of Islamic women in a patriarchal society. As Kia indicates, Âkhundzâde found occasion in his plays to "criticize every facet of traditional Muslim life in Iran and Transcaucasia, including corruption, superstition, exploitation and ignorance."[59] The authors of *The True Dream* must have been familiar with such plays.

Another form of drama, which has certainly influenced the authors of *The True Dream*, is the traditional Persian passion plays (*taʿziyye*), in which the life and death of Shiite saints, especially the martyrdom of Hoseyn, the third Shiite Imam, are annually commemorated in Iran. Although the story of Hoseyn's martyrdom is without doubt the most famous passion play, Persian *taʿziyye* possess a rich variety of subjects, including the history and legends of pre-Islamic Persia, Biblical and Koranic hagiographies, and even comic genres. This comic genre, *contradictio in terminis* in the context of the passion play, is exemplified by a black Ethiopian servant, called Qanbar, who cynically ridicules Hoseyn's adversaries and makes the audience laugh at the enemies of the Shiite Islam.[60] *The True Dream* treats a serious theme, the tyranny of the clergy and the government, in a startlingly humorous way.

Works cited

Abrahamian, E., *Iran between Two Revolutions*, Princeton: Princeton University Press, 1982.

Afary, J., *The Iranian Constitutional Revolution, 1906–1911: Grassroots Democracy, Social Democracy, and the Origins of Feminism*, New York: Columbia University Press, 1996.

Amanat, A., "The Historical Roots of the Persecution of Bâbis and Bâha'is in Iran," in *The Bâha'is of Iran: Socio-Historical Studies*, eds. D.P. Brookshaw and S.B. Fazel, London/New York: Routledge, 2008, pp. 170–183.

Âzâd Tabrizi, Hoseyn, *Les perles de la couronne*, Paris, 1903.

Âzâd Tabrizi, Hoseyn, *La roserarie du savoir/Golzār-e ma'refat*, 2 Vols., Paris and Leiden, 1906.

Âzâd Tabrizi, Hoseyn, *L'aube de l'espérance/Sobḥ-e ommid*, Paris and Leiden, 1909.

Âzâd Tabrizi, Hoseyn, *Guêpes et papillons*, Paris, 1916.

Bayat, M., *Mysticism and Dissent: Socioreligious Thought in Qajar Iran*, Syracuse: Syracuse University Press, 1982.

Bayat, M., *Iran's First Revolution, Shi'ism and the Constitutional Revolution of 1905–1909*, New York/Oxford: Oxford University Press, 1991.

Bearman, P., T. Bianquis, C.E. Bosworth, E. van Donzel, & W.P. Heinrichs, eds. *Encyclopaedia of Islam*, 2nd edition. Leiden: Brill, 1960–2005.

Browne, E.G., *The Persian Revolution of 1905–1909*, London: Frank Cass & Co., 1966.

Bruijn, J.T.P. de, "Other Persian Quatrains in Holland: The Roseraie du savoir of Ḥusayn-i Āzād," in *The Great 'Umar Khayyām: A Global Reception of the Rubáiyát*, ed. A.A. Seyed-Gohrab, Leiden: Leiden University Press, 2012, pp. 105–114.

Bruijn, J.T.P. de, in Yarshater, E., *Encyclopaedia Iranica* Encyclopaedia Iranica Foundation, 1987–. http://www.iranicaonline.org/, s.v. Āzād Tabrizi.

Cole, J.R.I., "Autobiography and Silence: The Early Career of Shaykh al-Ra'īs Qājār," in *Iran im 19. Jarhundert und die Entstehung der Bâha'i-Religion*, eds., J.C. Bürgel and I. Schayani, Zürich: Hildesheim (Religionswissenschaftliche Texte und Studien, Bd. 8), 1998, pp. 91–126.

Dadkhah, K.M., "Lebas-o Taqva: An Early Twentieth-Century Treatise on the Economy," in *Middle Eastern Studies*, Vol. 28, No. 3, 1992, pp. 547–558.

E'temâd al-Saltane, Mohammad Hasan Khan, *Kh^{w}âb-e Khalse (mashhur be kh^{w}âb-nâme)*, ed. by Mahmud Katirâ'i, Tehran: Tukâ, 2nd edition, 1978.

Fahd T., & H. Daiber, in Bearman, P. et al., eds. *Encyclopaedia of Islam*, 2nd edition. Leiden: Brill, 1960–2005, s.v. Ru'yā.

Fathi, A., "Role of the Traditional Leader in Modernization of Iran, 1890–1910," in *International Journal of Middle East Studies*, Vol. 11, No. 1, 1980, pp. 87–98.

Fathi, A., "The Culture and Social Structure of the Islamic Pulpit as a Medium of Communication in the Iranian Constitutional Revolution," in *Islamic Culture*, Vol. lxi, No. 4, 1987, pp. 28–45.

Fathi, A., "Ahmad Kasravi and Seyyed Jamal Waez on Constitutionalism in Iran," in *Middle Eastern Studies*, Vol. 29, No. 4, 1993, pp. 702–713.

Fathi, A., "Seyyed Jamal Vaez and the 'Aljamal' Newspaper in Iran," in *Middle Eastern Studies*, Vol. 33, No. 2, 1997, pp. 216–225.

Ghanoonparvar, M.R., in Yarshater, E., *Encyclopaedia Iranica*, Encyclopaedia Iranica Foundation, 1987–. http://www.iranicaonline.org/, s.v. Drama.

Haar, J.G.J., ter, "Ta'ziye: Ritual Theater from Shiite Iran," in *Theatre Intercontinental: Forms, Functions, Correspondences*, ed. by C.C. Barfoot & C. Bordewijk, Amsterdam: Rodopi, 1993, pp. 155–174.

Works cited

Jamâlzâde, Mohammad-Ali, *Sar-o tah yak karbâs yâ Esfahân-nâma*, Tehran: Âtashkade 1955.

Jamâlzâde, Mohammad-Ali, *Isfahan is Half the World: Memories of a Persian Boyhood*, (Translation of *Sar-o tah yek karbâs*), by W.L. Heston, Princeton: Princeton University Press, 1983.

Kasravi, A., *Târikh-e mashrute-ye Irân*, Tehran: Negâh, 3rd edition, 1385/2006.

Katouzian, H., *The Persians: Ancient, Medieval and Modern Iran*, New Haven/London: Yale University Press, 2009.

Katouzian, H., "Seyyed Hasan Taqizadeh: Three Lives in a Lifetime," in *Iran: Politics, History and Literature*, London/New York: Routledge, 2013.

Katouzian, H., "Satire in Persian Literature 1900–1940," in *Literature of the Early Twentieth Century from the Constitutional Period to Reza Shah*, ed. Ali-Asghar Seyed-Gohrab, London and New York: I.B. Tauris, 2015, pp. 161–239.

Keddie, N.R., in Yarshater, E., *Encyclopaedia Iranica*, Encyclopaedia Iranica Foundation, 1987–. http://www.iranicaonline.org/, s.v. Afghānī, Jamāl-al-dīn.

Kermâni, Nâzem-al-Eslâm, *Târikh-e bidâri-ye irâniyân*, Tehran: Amir Kabir, 1999.

Kia, M., "Constitutionalism, Economic Modernization and Islam in the Writings of Mirzâ Yusef Khan Mostashar od-Dowle," in *Middle Eastern Studies*, Vol. 30, No. 4, 1994, pp. 751–777.

Kia, M., "Women, Islam and Modernity in Akhundzade's Plays and Unpublished Writings," in *Middle Eastern Studies*, Vol. 34, No. 3, 1998, pp. 1–33.

Kiliç, E., *The Balkan War (1912–1913) and Visions of the Future in Ottoman Turkish Literature*, PhD dissertation, Leiden University, 2015.

Lorey, Eustache de, & Douglas Sladen, *The Moon of the Fourteenth Night: Being the Private Life of an Unmarried Diplomat in Persia during the Revolution*, London: Hurst & Blackett, 1910.

Marâghe'i, Zeyn-al-'Âbedin, *The Travel Diary of Ebrahim Beg by Zayn ol-'Abedin Maraghe'i*, trans. by James D. Clark, Costa Mesa, CA: Mazda Publishers, 2006.

Martin, V., *The Qajar Pact: Bargaining, Protest and the State in Nineteenth-Century Persia*, London/New York: I.B. Tauris, 2005.

Martin, V., "Aqa Najafi, Haj Aqa Nurullah, and the Emergence of Islamism in Isfahan, 1889–1908," in *Iranian Studies*, Vol. 41.2, 2008, pp. 155–172.

Momen, M., "The Constitutional Movement and the Bâha'is of Iran: The Creation of an 'Enemy Within' in British," in *Journal of Middle Eastern Studies*, Vol. 39, No. 3, 2012, pp. 328–346.

Mozaffari, N., in Yarshater, E., *Encyclopaedia Iranica*, Encyclopaedia Iranica Foundation, 1987–. http://www.iranicaonline.org/, s.v. Jamalzadeh, Mohammad-Ali. i. Life.

Nâteq, H., *Kâr-nâme va zamâne-ye Mirzâ Rezâ Kermâni*, no place of publication: Afra, 1984.

Nicolas, A.L.M., *Massacres de Bâbis en Perse*, Paris: Adrien Maisonneuve, 1936.

Osborn L., in *Religion and Relevance: The Bahâ'îs in Britain, 1899–1933*, Studies in the Bâbî and Bahâ'î Religions vol. 24, Los Angeles: Kalimat Press, 2014.

Parvin, N., in Yarshater, E., *Encyclopaedia Iranica*, Encyclopaedia Iranica Foundation, 1987–. http://www.iranicaonline.org/, s.v. Bīdārī.

Ridgeon, L. *Sufi Castigator: Ahmad Kasravi and the Iranian Mystical Tradition*, London/New York: Routledge, 2006.

Royâ-ye sâdeqe (der Warhaftige Truam, Le Rêve Sincère), übersetzt und überarbeitet von B. Choubiné, Enteshârât-e mard-e Emruz, 1986.

Rumi, Jalâl al-Din, *Mathnavi*, Vol. III, ed. M. Este'lâmi, Tehran: Zavvâr, 1993.

Ruz-nâme-ye E'temâd al-Saltaneh, ed. I. Afshar, Tehran: 'Elmi, 2nd edition, 1971.
Sadeghian, S., "Minorities and Foreigners in a Provincial Iranian City: Bahā'is in the Russian Consulate of Isfahan in 1903," in *Journal of Persianate Studies*, Vol. 9, 2016, pp. 107–132.
Sadiq, 'Isâ, *Yâdgar-e 'omr: khâterâti az sargozasht-e doctor 'Isâ Sadiq ke az lahâz-e tarbiyyat sudmand tavânad bud*, vol. I, Tehran: Sherkat-e Sahâmi-ye Tab'-e ketâb, 1961.
Sayyâh, Hâjj Mohammad-Ali Mahallâti, *An Iranian in Nineteenth Century Europe: The Travel Diaries of Hâjj Sayyâh 1859–1877*, trans. by Mehrbanoo Nasser Deyhim, Bethesda, MD: Ibex Publishers, 1998.
Seyed-Gohrab, A.A., "Modern Persian Prose and Fiction Between 1900 and 1940," in *Literature of the Early Twentieth Century: From the Constitutional Period to Reza Shah*, ed. A.A. Seyed-Gohrab, Volume XI of A History of Persian Literature, London/New York: I.B. Tauris 2015, pp. 133–160.
Seyed-Gohrab, A.A., & S. McGlinn, *One Word – Yak kaleme: 19th-century Persian Treatise Introducing Western Codified Law*, Leiden: Leiden University Press, 2010.
Sparroy, W., *Persian Children of the Royal Family: The Narrative of an English Tutor at the Court of H.I.H. Zillu's-Sultán*, London/New York: John Lane, 1902.
Talajooy, S., "A History of Iranian Drama (1850 to 1941)," in *Literature of the Early Twentieth Century: From the Constitutional Period to Reza Shah*, Volume XI, ed., Ali-Asghar Seyed-Gohrab, London/New York: I.B. Tauris, 2015, pp. 353–410.
The Moon of the Fourteenth Night: Being the Private Life of an Unmarried Diplomat in Persia during the Revolution, made into a book by Eustache de Lorey and Doughlas Sladen, London: Hurst & Blackett, 1910.
Walcher, H., in Yarshater, E., *Encyclopaedia Iranica*, Encyclopaedia Iranica Foundation, 1987–. http://www.iranicaonline.org/, s.v. Isfahan, iii. Population, iii (1). The Qajar Period.
Walcher, H.A., *In the Shadow of the King: Zell al-Sultan and Isfahan under the Qajars*, London/New York: I.B. Tauris, 2008.
Yaghmâ'i, E., *Shahid-e Âzâdi: Seyyed Jamâl Wâ'ez Esfahâni*, Tehran: Tus, 1978.
Yarshater, E., *Encyclopaedia Iranica*, Encyclopaedia Iranica Foundation, 1987–. http://www.iranicaonline.org/, s.v.v. Bābism, Azali Bābism, Bāhaism, Bahā'-Allāh and 'Abd-al-Bahā.
Zell al-Soltân, Mirzâ Mas'ud, *Târikh-e Mas'udi*, Tehran: Yasâwoli, 1983.
Ziai, H., in Yarshater, E., *Encyclopaedia Iranica*, Encyclopaedia Iranica Foundation, 1987–. http://www.iranicaonline.org/, s.v. Dreams and Dream Interpretation. ii. In the Persian Tradition.

The True Dream

It had been a hard day. The pressure of my daily work, the many discussions, and a multiplicity of events and meetings with friends and foes – all this had sucked me from the coast of strength into the whirlpool of powerlessness and helplessness. My fatigue was boundless, and this weakness persisted until in the early evening the bounty of sleep arrived, and stupefaction snatched away my restlessness.

As it happened, strange events and observations were also presented to me in the world of my dreams. I saw the world of the Assembly and Ranking of souls. I wandered in the wilderness of terror and in the infinite plain of the Resurrection. It was just like the illustrations and explanations given for it in the Islamic traditions and in pious stories, but a hundred times more so.

For some time I was in a state of amazement and agitation, and deep thought. What would they do to me? What chastisements would my weak body suffer? I clung to the robe of every passer-by and sought my deliverance at every refuge. All I got from those I asked was the cry of "Alas, my soul" and the lament of "confounded by blame!"

While this was going on, I remembered that His Excellency the Reverend Seyyed Abu Ja'far – may God the Exalted bless him – who was the religious leader in the quarter of the city where we lived had on several occasions personally intervened to settle issues; he would steer them to himself to collect some share for his sons

رؤیای صادقه

اول شبی که روز آن از شدت مشاغل و مکاسب و ازدیاد گفت و شنود و بسیاری حوادث و مشاهده دوست و عنود بکلی از سواحل توانائی به غرقاب ناتوانی و گرداب بی پارگی فرورفته خستگی از حد گذشت و درد ضعف ممتد گشت، که نعمت خواب رسید و بهت بیتابی را در ربود.

بر حسب اتفاق در آن عالم رویا نیز مشاهدات و معاینات عجیب درافتاده عوالم حشر و مراتب نشر را می‌دیدم و در صحرای وحشت و فضای لایتناهی قیامت سیر توضیح و تشریح و بنای آن چنانچه در احادیث و اخبارات خبر داده‌اند چنان می‌کردم . بود، بلکه صد چندان

مدتی در تحیر و تفکر و تزلزل بودم که آیا با من چه خواهند کرد و این بدن ضعیف را در چه مؤاخذات خواهند آورد. دست به هر دامنی می‌زدم و تمنی نجات از هر مؤمنی می‌خواستم

تمام صداها وانفسا جوابم بود و فریاد واحیرتا عتاب. در ضمن به خیال افتادم که جناب مستطاب شریعتمدار آقای آقا سید ابوجعفر سلمه‌الله تعالی که در محلۀ مسکونی خودمان در دنیا ریاست روحانی داشتند، بارها در ختم و انجام مسائل راجعه به این بنده به طرف خود می غلطیدند که سهمی برای آقازادگان منظور می‌داشتند

and he had assured me that, in exchange, he would intercede with his ancestor (Mohammad) for me in the next world and secure his forgiveness for me. I needed to find him straight away and remind him of what had occurred in the material world so that he could do something, and He might show mercy, that I might be freed, that some remedy might be found.

After a long search and much speaking [I found him]. He said: "Leave me alone. I'm like you, looking for someone who could introduce me to my ancestor, to help me out of my own difficulty."

I looked around and saw a huge crowd around Seyyed Abu Jafar. I supposed they were simply petitioning for a position in the service of God, to serve His splendour, magnificence, sublimity and benevolence. When I looked more closely, I realized that all these people were there with pleas, writs and demands. The poor gentleman was a hundred times deeper than I in the sea of fear and bewilderment. This discovery increased my fear and confusion a thousand-fold. Moreover, this boundless desert was filled by an innumerable jostling horde, and the burning earth and scorching sun were blazing and boiling every atom of my existence moment by moment. I was perplexed beyond measure when I thought of the grace of God and His mercy.

In the distance, among the various groups and countless millions, I saw Mirzâ Mohammad Khan Nâzem-al-Khalvat the Chamberlain. He also saw me, and shouted to me: "Mr. so-and-so![61] What are you doing here? Can't you see what a donkey market it is here?" "I'm perishing!" I replied. "If only someone could think of a way out and show me."

"Be calm; do not be afraid of this huge crowd, they are only worthless, idle so-and-so's." Taking me by the hand, he led me to a spot that was slightly elevated, and told me, "When they call your name, you must appear before the scales of justice; apart from that, nobody

و مرا به آن تسلیت میدادند که در آخرت به عوض در حضور جدم شفاعت میکنم و عنایتت می‌بخشم. فوراً ایشان را بیابم و یادآور عوالم دنیوی شوم که کاری فرمایند و ترحمی نمایند شاید استخلاص حاصل شود و به استعلاجی واصل گردم

پس از جستجوی زیاد و گفتگوی بسیار، جواب فرمود: برو بابا من خود در پی مثل تونی هستم که معرفی مرا نزد جدم نموده شاید از گرفتاریهای خود خلاصی یابم. اطراف آقا را نگریستم جمع کثیری دیدم حمل نمودم شاید محض تجمل و تجلل و مرحمت از طرف خداوندی به مأموریت استخدام ایشانند

خوب متعمقانه نگریستم معلوم شد این جمعیت هر یک با دعا و کلامی مدعی و طلبکارند بیچاره آقا در دریای وحشت و حیرت صد چندان بدتر از من غوطه ور است. این مشاهده و مکاشفه هزار بار بر ترس و سرگردانیم افزود و در این صحرای بی منتها که از هر گوشه غوغا و ازدحامی لاتعد و لاتحصی بود زمین سوزان و آفتاب گدازان هر دقیقه و آنی وجود را پخته و سوخته میداشت. بی اندازه پریشان شده بودم که فضل الهی و ترحم ربانی شامل آمد .

از دور در میان گروهات مختلفه و کرورات متعدده میرزا محمد خان ناظم خلوت را مشاهده کرده مشارالیه نیز نظرش به من افتاد. صدا بلند کرد: ای فلانی اینجا چکار می‌کنی مگر نمی‌بینی چه خربازاری است. گفتم فلانی فکری کن و راهی بنما که هلاک شدم. گفت: بیخیال باش جمعیت زیاد را وحشت مکن همه اینها زیردمیشان سست است، و دست مرا گرفته در گوشه‌ای که جزئی ارتفاع داشت، گفت: بایست تا هروقت اسم ترا خواندند در پای میزان حساب حاضر شوی والا کسی را

will do anything to you."

Standing there, the spectacle of that boundless plain and of God's diverse creation was spread before me. My bewilderment was so immeasurable that I cannot describe it, and my fear so great that no pen could record it. People of many nations, from countless cities, were continually appearing before the scales of justice. At each moment, a Herald would cry out a certain call, until I heard a Herald call out in Persian: "Isfahan."

Hearing the name of my homeland, a trembling took hold of my body. I strained my ears and turned my attention towards the scales of justice.

A Herald announced the ulama. They brought forward a group of gentlemen, and were rebuking and punishing them. I did not recognize them, or know of them, until, from the court of the Lord of Lords, the Herald cried, "Sheykh Mohammed Baqer, Mojtahed of Esfahan!" I saw that they led his Eminence, the Hojjato'l-Islam, before the scales of justice. All the people were sending cries of 'Peace and Blessings' after him.[62] The Voice from on High[63] said: "O Sheykh! Today is the day of punishment, and also of retribution. Give answers to our questions truthfully, one by one, and pay the reckoning for your life in the world, dinar for dinar."

The Sheykh's tears were flowing as he replied in utter anguish: "O God! Were it not for your overlooking [my faults], and your mercy, what a position I would be in!"

The Voice replied: "O Sheykh, now when you've come with your shortcomings to our place, and bring your lowly supplications, it is ours to ask questions. We refer the matter to your own fair-mindedness. You sit in judgement and determine your own punishment."

با تو کاری نیست.
در آن نقطه ایستاده تماشای آن صحرای لایتناهی و مخلوقات مختلفه الهی می‌نمودم. تحیر باندازه ایست که بیانش محال است و توحش بقدری که تقریر و عنوانش ممکن نیست. دائماً شخص و افراد ممالک عدیده و شهرهای بعیده را در پای میزان حساب می‌آوردند. هر وقت منادی به صدائی فریاد می‌نمود تا شنیدم منادی به زبان ایرانی فریاد کرد اصفهان
اسم وطن را شنیدم لرزه به اندامم افتاد. گوشها را تیز و هوش را به طرف میزان متوجه نمودم
منادی ندا در داد علماء. جمعی از آقایان را آوردند، مؤاخذات کردند و مجازات دادند که نمی‌شناختم و نمی‌دانستم تا از درگاه رب الرباب منادی ندا داد شیخ محمد باقر مجتهد اصفهانی مشاهده کردم جناب مستطاب حجت الاسلام را که به احترامی تمام در حالتیکه تمام مردم و اتباع دائماً سلام و صلوات در پشت سر آقا میفرستادند، به پای میزان حساب آوردند. خطاب مستطاب رسید: ای شیخ امروز روز مجازات است و هنگام مکافات. سئوالات ما را جواب صحیح یک یک باید بدهی و حساب دنیا را دینار دینار باید بپردازی
اشک شیخ جاری شد و با اضطرابی تمام عرض کرد: الهی اگر ترحم و اغماض تو نباشد پس وای به احوال من .
خطاب: ای شیخ کنون که به مقام عجز ما آمدی و تضرع آوردی سئوالاتی است، رجوع به انصاف خودت می‌نمائیم جواب و کیفر آنها را نیز

He said: "What option is there for a weak creature, except to submit and accept?"

The Voice asked: "O Sheykh, have you lacked any bounties and favours in the world?"

"None."

"Were your training and knowledge proportionate to your power?"

"No."

"Did you suffer any wretchedness or grief?"

"No."

"Were your understanding and reason diminished?"

"No."

"Were you despised and undervalued among the ulama?"

"No."

"Did you not have an agreeable wife, which is a large part of happiness?"

"Yes."

"Did you not have many strong and pious children?"

"Yes."

"Did we not give you the power and inclination to show benevolence to people?"

"Yes."

"Did we not give you the power to pass verdicts?"

"Yes."

"Were you not respected by the king and state officials, did you not have an influential voice?"

"Yes."

"If you had wanted to serve the Muslim community and increase their well-being, would you not have had the opportunity to do so?"

"Yes."

"So you had every kind of capability?"

"Yes."

"We seek your own fair judgement, then: in the light of all these bounties from us, how have you served our servants and the Muslims?" He remained silent.

"What oppression have you eliminated?" Sweat broke out on his forehead.

"How many institutions of public benefit have you established?" ...

"How many orphanages have you built?" He lowered his head.

"How many shelters for the exiles?" He burst into tears.

خودت بیان کن. عرض کرد بنده ضعیفی جز تمکین و رضا چه چاره دارد.
خطاب: ای شیخ آیا در دنیا تفضلات و عنایات چیزی برای تو ناقص گذاشت؟
جواب: خیر.
خطاب: آیا سواد و علم تو به درجهٔ اقتدارت بود؟
جواب: خیر.
خطاب: ادراک و عقلت کاستی داشت؟
جواب: خیر.
خطاب: در میان علماء حقیر و خفیف داشتمت؟
جواب: خیر.
خطاب: زوجهٔ مطبوعه که عمدهٔ سعادتست نداشتی؟
جواب: چرا.
خطاب: اولاد رشید عدیدهٔ توانا نداشتی؟
جواب: چرا.
خطاب: عزت و توجه نفوس مرحمت نکردیم؟
جواب: چرا.
خطاب: نفوذ احکام به تو ندادیم؟
جواب: چرا.
خطاب: نزد سلطان و حکام محترم و نافذالقول نبودی؟
جواب: چرا.
خطاب: اگر خدمت و بنای خیر و منافع عامه مسلمانان را می‌خواستی به جا بیاوری نمی‌توانستی؟
جواب: چرا.
خطاب: پس همه نوع اقتدار داشتی؟
جواب: بلی.
خطاب: از خودت انصاف می‌خواهیم. آیا در مقابل این نعمتهای ما چه خدمتی به بندگان و مسلمانان ما کردی؟
جواب: سکوت.
خطاب: رفع کدام ظلم نمودی؟
جواب: عرق پیشانی.
خطاب: کدام بنای خیر عمومی را نهادی؟
جواب: ...
خطاب: چند یتیم خانه بنا کردی؟
جواب: گردن کج.
خطاب: چند غریب خانه را بانی شدی؟
جواب: اشک جاری.

"O Sheykh, our willingness to close our eyes exceeds the imagination and the sins of our creatures. If we rebuked you for all of these, your fear and shame would pain even us. Do you yourself know what crime you committed at the rebellion of 1296 (1879 AD) in Esfahan and how many of our servants you plunged into affliction and suffering?"

The mere mention of the rebellion of 1879 was enough to cause an extraordinary shaking to run through the Sheykh's body. He turned pale; he could no longer stand on his feet. Fear and terror made him sink to the ground; his soul left his body. I saw that the heat and burning of that desert had turned his blessed body to ash. All those who were looking at this were overwhelmed with fear. A huge tumult rose from the Plain of Assembly. From the Fountainhead of Glory came the command: "Let the people be silent!" Then the ashes of the Sheykh were summoned: "O Sheykh! Rise and give answers, because today is the Day of Reckoning."

Instantly I saw that handful of ashes return to their previous state. His honour the Sheykh responded in plaintive tones. "Lord! Ignorance and negligence are the cause of all transgressions."

The Voice said, "O Sheykh! We have strengthened your heart so that you can answer our questions in a measured and eloquent way, otherwise you will be severely punished."

"My God, I'll do as you command," he replied.

The Voice asked, "Were you not informed about the oppression and transgressions of the government and its officers?"

"I was."

"Did you not know the reason for the rebellion (of 1879)?"

"I did."

"Did you not make a solemn agreement with the ulama of Isfahan and in particular with Mir Mohammad Hoseyn, the Friday prayer leader? Did you not swear that you would not rest until you had put an end to the government's oppressions?"

"I did."

خطاب: اغماض ما یا شیخ بیش از تصورات و خطاهای بندگان است. اگر جملگی را مؤاخذه نمائیم وحشت و خجلت تو ما را متألم خواهد نمود. آیا در واقعه بلوای ۱۲۹۶ اصفهان تو خود میدانی چه خلافی کردی و چقدر بندگان ما را در عذاب و گرفتاری انداختی؟

اسم شورش سنه ۱۲۹۶ را به محضی که شیخ استماع فرمودند لرزه فوق العاده بر اندامشان افتاده رنگ رخسارشان پریده روی پا نتوانستند بایستند از وحشت و اضطراب به زمین افتاده روح از جسمشان خارج شده حالت گرما و سوزندگی آن صحرا بدن مبارکشان را دیدم خاکستر ساخت. تمام نظاره کنندگان از این حال متوحش شده غوغای عظیمی از صفحه محشر برخاست. از مصدر جلال امر به سکوت عامه گردید و ندائی به خاکستر شیخ داده شد که یا شیخ برخیز و جواب بازگوی که امروز روز جزاست . فوراً دیدم آن مشت خاکستر به حالت اولیه خود عود کرد و به آهنگ سوزناکی جناب شیخ جواب دادند:

جواب: الهی نادانی و تغافل است که باعث هر عصیانی می شود.

خطاب: یا شیخ دل تو را محکم گردانیدیم که جواب خطابات ما را شمرده و فصیح بدهی والا مورد عتاب سخت خواهی شد

جواب: پروردگارا آنچه فرمائی چنان کنم.

خطاب: آیا تعدی و اجحاف حکومت و اجزای آن را نمی‌دانستی؟

جواب: چرا.

خطاب: آیا جهت آن بلوا را نفهمیدی؟

جواب: چرا.

خطاب: آیا با علمای اصفهان و مخصوصاً میرمحمد حسین امام جمعه عهد و میثاق نبستید، قسم یاد ننمودید که تا رفع تعدی اجزای حکومت را نکنید دست بردار نشوید؟

جواب: چرا.

"Were you not, yourself, the instigator and promoter of that insurrection?"

"I was."

"Is it true that this insurrection was due to the cruelty of Ja'far Qoli Khan and Mohammad-'Ali Khan, the general supervisor and Minister, who had imposed a heavy grain tax on the population? Wasn't your purpose low food prices and the elimination of the tyranny of government officers and, along with that, to achieve a tranquil life for yourself?"

"Yes," he answered.

"Then why did you side with Zell-al-Soltân Mas'ud Mirzâ and betray your promise? You put certain people in grave danger. You left the Friday Imam, Mirzâ Hoseyn, dishonoured and all alone. In fact, you caused him to die of a broken heart and, by putting him in grave danger, purely out of your enmity for him, you have also made life a misery for these Muslims."

"O God," he replied, "you are my witness that he insulted me. One of the things he did was to order that Mulla Mohammad Naqneh, who was accused of having slandered him, should be dragged from my house, and carried away. They treated him like a beast. Is there a greater humiliation and enmity than this? Moreover, he has continually wronged me, just for the sake of his own reputation and authority. You are a better witness and more informed. Why should I explain what is clear?"

The Voice said, "So your sole purpose was only your own benefit and the satisfaction of your base desires! Bravo! You have taken excellent care of my laws, and of the Muslims! Do you know how much loss your disagreement in the day of rebellion caused to the Muslims and the poor, and how much your betrayal has cost them, to this day?"

"O God," he replied, "you are the Knowing and the Wise, from the beginning to the end of the world. How can I know my own errors?"

"If you had not raised a dispute on that day about lifting the taxes on the Muslims' grain and bread, they would not be hoarding thousands of tons of grain for your children today. The rotten grain

خطاب: مگر اصل و بنیان آن شورش را تو خود برپا نکردی؟
جواب: چرا.
خطاب: مگر نه آن بلوا را برای تعدی جعفر قلیخان و محمد علیخان که ضابط کل و وزیر بود و وزیر بود و گندم را به تسعیر گران تحمیل اهالی می‌نمودند و مگر نه مقصود شما ارزانی ارزاق و رفع اجحاف اجزای حکومت و ضمناً رفاهیت حال خود را هم مقصود داشتید؟
جواب: چرا.
خطاب: پس چرا با ظل السلطان مسعود میرزا ساختی و پای خود را عقب کشیدی گروهی را در مهلکه انداختی میرحسین امام جمعه را مفتضح و تنها کردی. او را در واقع تو دق دادی و به مهلکه انداختی محض عداوتی که با او داشتی این همه مسلمانان را به صعوبت انداختی .
جواب: الهی تو خود هم گواهی که او هم توهین مرا نمود، یکی از کارهایش آنکه ملا محمد نقنه را که متهم به بد گفتن او شده بود فرستاد از منزل من کشیدند و بردند ، آخورش بستند. توهین از بالاتر و عداوتی از این بدتر چه بوده؟ گذشته از آن، دائماً محض ترویج و اقتدار خود با من بدها کرد. تو بهتر گواهی و خوبتر آگاهی آنجا که عیان است چه حاجت به بیان است .
خطاب: پس این حرکات تو از نظر شخصانی و هوای نفسانی بوده. مرحبا خوب شریعت مرا نگهداری و مسلمانان را پاس داری کرده‌ای. هیچ می دانی که مخالفت آنروز تو چه ضررها به مسلمین و فقرا زده چه خیانتها که تا امروز نموده؟
جواب: خدایا توئی عالم و دانای اولین و آخرین. من چه خبر از خطای خود دارم.
خطاب: اگر آنروز برای عدم تحمیلات غله و نان مسلمانان آن مخالفت را تو نمی‌کردی امروز از اولاد خودت غله را هزار خروار انبار و احتکار نمی‌کردند. غله پوسیده از

would not be dumped from their stores into the river, five hundred loads at a time. The Islamic jurists and ulama would not have been known as 'The Rich,' so that they are seen as the cause of the poverty of the poor and the weakness of the weak. It is prosperity and wealth that must be closely examined and scrutinized, to implement the commands of God and do justice to the rights of Muslims, whereas the contrary course of action has been taken."

While these words were being spoken, the groans and cries of the poor, the oppressed and the helpless were raised, saying: "O God, do not let the oppressors decide our fate. What sufferings we have borne in the world, how much we have suffered from hunger, how many rebukes we have borne." As a result of their crying, the earth in the Place of Assembly began to tremble, and all the people on that plain fell into a strange state. After that trembling and uproar, they were dumbfounded.

Then God's threatening voice was heard, saying, "O Sheykh, what response do you have for our creatures? For if they make one more complaint, you will find yourself in everlasting punishment."

I saw that the Sheykh was in such a pitiful condition that some of the people in the Assembly pitied him too. In utter humility and submission, he replied, "My God, I have something to say, but shame prevents me, and apprehension holds me back. I'm afraid that it might be unsuitable for the court of divinity and provoke your wrath."

The Voice said, "O Sheykh! Today is not the day to hang back and consider! Our court is not a place where you may suffer chastisement and punishments for no reason. Say what you have to say, and present whatever answer you may have."

"My God, I'm afraid that you might not look on me with grace and mercy, I fear you may chastise me according to your justice. O God, for the sake of your Near Ones, grant this poor servant your compassion and listen to my humble words."

The Voice said, "Say no more, but give me your answer."

انبارشان به رودخانه پانصد بار پانصد بار ریخته نمی‌شد. مجتهدین و علما این سمت اعیانیت و تمول پیدا نمی‌کردند که باعث فقر فقرا و ضعفا شوند، دارائی و تمول است که ملاحظه و تأمل در اجرای احکام الهی و احقاق حقوق مسلمین می‌آورد و از برای اجرای باطل را باعث می‌شود.

در اثنای این خطاب ناله و فریاد و صدائی از مظلومین و فقرا و بیچارگان بلند شد که: الهی داد ما را از ظالمین بگیر که در دنیا چه زجرها بردیم و چه گرسنگیها و سرزنشها کشیدیم که زمین محضر به لرزه در آمد و حالت غریبی تمام اهل آن صحرا را دست داد و بعد از آن لرزه و غوغا بهت و مات عجیبی عارض شد.

خطاب تهدیدانه رسید که:

خطاب: ای شیخ جواب بندگان ما را چه می‌گوئی که اگر یک شکایت دیگر کنند در عذاب مؤبد خواهی بود.

دیدم شیخ حالت رقتی عارضش شد که بعضی از اهل محشر نیز به رقت آمدند. با کمال خضوع و لابه عرض کرد:

جواب: الهی عرض دارم، خجلت مانع است و وحشت نمی‌گذارد عرض نمایم. می‌ترسم به درگاه خداوندیت ناپسند آید و موجب غضب شود.

خطاب: یا شیخ امروز روزی نیست که توحش و ملاحظه نمائی و درگاه ما بارگاهی نیست که بی جهت عذاب و اذیتی ببینی. آنچه خواهی و هست بازگوی و هر جوابی داری آغاز کن.

جواب: بارالها از آن هر اسانم که مبادا به فضل و ترحم نظر نفرمائی و به عدل تنبیه و عذاب فرمائی. خداوندا به دوستان آستانت که به این عبد ذلیل ترحم فرما و به سخنان عاجزانه‌اش تعمق نما.

خطاب: بیش از این تکرار مکن و آنچه جواب صوابست بیان کن.

"My God," he replied, "was I anything more than a human being on earth? Did I have a sanctified soul? Did you appoint me to be a prophet, a messenger or an imam?"

"No."

"My God, was I not caught in the whirlpool and waves of the sea of lust and bodily passions?"

"Yes."

"Have I not made efforts to repel devilish temptations and to protect the outward forms of the religious law?"

"Yes."

"Have I not shown heartfelt thankfulness and satisfaction with your various bounties?"

"Yes."

"Then, my God, with all frankness and complete candour I will reply, and I ask your approval. If, instead of this weak and poor servant, one of the Angels of Nearness or one of your Messengers or…"

God replied: "Do not be afraid; rather, tell us what is in your heart. This is not the place for looking after your own interests or dissimulation."

The Sheykh then completed his plea, "May God protect me, if God himself were dressed in human form, and you were appointed as the ruler and judge in religious and civil matters in Isfahan, in light of the various deceptions, innumerable regulations and preparations for countless intrigues of his Excellency, the great, the Exalted, the Holy, the redoubtable Zel-ul-Soltân, what would you do? Would you not be deceived?"

During this exchange, all the people of Esfahan present there, the people of the world, the well informed and knowledgeable, shouted with one voice in chorus, pleading: "O God, the Sheykh is telling the truth! Of all that he has said, this is the best. We are witnesses to it."

The reply came, "O Sheykh, if this their testimony had not been given today, you would have been severely punished, and suffered endlessly. But now, our forgiveness and compassion is

عرض: خدایا، آیا من در دنیا بشری بیش بودم؟ آیا من نفس قدسی داشتم؟ آیا سمت نبوت یا رسالت یا امامت مرحمت فرموده بودی؟
جواب: نه.
عرض: بار پروردگارا، آیا گرفتار تلاطمها و امواج دریای شهوت و خواهشهای نفسانی نبودم؟
جواب: چرا.
عرض: آیا در مدافعهٔ وساوس شیطانی و نگاهداری ظاهر شرع خود سعی و کوشش نداشتم؟
جواب: چرا.
عرض: آیا خوشنودی و تشکر قلبی از نعمتهای گوناگون تو نمی‌نمودم؟
جواب: چرا.
عرض: پس الهی با کمال جرأت و نهایت مروت عرض می‌کنم و تصدیق می‌خواهم. اگر به عوض این بندهٔ ضعیف و عبد ذلیل یکی از ملائکه مقرب یا پیغمبران مرسل یا آآآلللل....
خطاب: مترس دیگر آنچه در دل داری بگو. اینجا آستان غرض و اغماض نیست.
تتمیم عرض:
یا العیاذبک. اگر خود حضرت خداوندیت به لباس بشریت به حکومت و قضاوت شرعی و ملی اصفهان مسند نشین و مقرر بودی، با آن فریبهای گوناگون و تدبیرات از حد افزون و زمینه سازی و تدلیسات از اندازه بیرون حضرت مستطاب امجد ارفع اقدس امنع والا ظل السلطان اروحنا فداه چه می‌کردی، آیا فریب نمی‌خوردی؟
در این ضمن تمام حضار محضر از اصفهانیان و عالمیان و مطلعین دفعهٔ واحده با صدایی بلند و آوازی مخلوط با تضرع فریاد کردند که: الهی شیخ راست می‌گوید و از تمام اقوال او این را بهتر می‌دانیم و شهادت می‌دهیم.
خطاب رسید که:
یا شیخ اگر این شهادت نامه نبود امروز به شدت سخط و نهایت عذاب ما واصل می شدی ولی اکنون با این حال عفو و اغماض ترحم ما شامل حالت شده

yours. As of now, you will not be punished, but we will not bestow on you our favour and reward."

Tears began to pour from the eyes of the Sheykh, and fell to the burning soil of the Plain of Resurrection. With the utmost humility he beseeched God, "My God, I'm fearful and anxious that they will not fulfil your generous promise and will prevent you from upholding your compassionate verdict. I fear that you will, nevertheless, severely punish me. O God, this body has been cherished by your innumerable bounties, it cannot bear the severity of your wrath."

"O Sheykh! Our forgiveness and compassion will not be taken back. Put your mind at rest."

"If the abuser allows it, my God."

"O Sheykh! Tell us the reason for your fear; why so agitated?"

"O God, in your court I can only speak truly and sincerely. Whatever fears I may have, I take refuge in you. I seek shelter under your pure grandeur. The man whom I have mentioned certainly has collaborators everywhere. Even here, on the Plain, he has his informers. I'm afraid that he will hear of these doings and do whatever he can to poison your mind about this, your humble servant, or that he will stir up the people on this Plain to rebel against me, so that each of them, with words or other things at other stages, will importune me, and I will eternally be a captive and suffer as a result."

"O Sheykh! As for the human understanding, it is true that it is limited and you have more regard for the fear and apprehension of God than for your own understanding. For we see that all of your kind are fearful, and subject to God, but it is clear that you still do not have complete understanding of the ranks of our divinity. Everyone, whether Zell-al-Soltân or any prince or nobleman, is subjected, submissive, humiliated and weak in relation to our divine Decree. Is this why you have mentioned his name in our court with so much respect?"

علی العجاله نه به عذابی معذبت می‌داریم و نه به عنایت و ثوابی مفتخرت می‌سازیم.
اشک شیخ جاری شد و به خاک سوزان محشر افتاده با نهایت عجز و انکسار عرض الهی می ترسم و وحشت دارم که به وعدۀ کریمانه‌ات نگذارند رفتار نمائی و از این رأی رحیمانه‌ات بازدارند که باز سخط و عذابم فرمائی. الهی این بدن به نعمتهای وافرت ناز پرورده شده طاقت شدتهای غضبت را ندارد.
خطاب: یا شیخ، عفو و اغماض ما بازگشت ندارد، خاطر آسوده دار.
جواب: بارالها اگر مفسد بگذارد.
خطاب: یا شیخ بگو وحشتت از چیست و اضطرابت به چه سبب است؟
جواب: خدایا در درگاه تو جز صدق و راستی نمی‌توانم عرضی نمایم و هر هراسی که دارم بتو باید پناه آور شوم و پناه به عزت پاکت عرض می‌نمایم. شخص سابق الذکر لابد در هر نقطه مفتش و در این صحرا هم در هر گوشه اخبارنگاری دارد. می‌ترسم که از واقعه مستحضر گردد و به هر قسم تدبیری که باشد خاطر خداوندیت را از این عبد ذلیل برنجاند و یا ازدحام محشر را بر ضدم بشوراند که باز هر یک به حرفی یا هر کدام به مقامی پاپیچم شوند و باعث گرفتاری و عذاب ابدیم گردند.
خطاب: ای شیخ ادراک شما نوع بشر صحیح است که محدود است و وحشت و ترس از ما یک مرتبه بالاتر از ادراک خودید که همه نوع مضطرب و مقهور او هستید، ولی معلوم است که هنوز شناسائی کامل در مراتب الوهیت ما پیدا نکرده‌اید که نوع انسان، خواه ظل السلطان خواه هر شاهزاده و خانی باشد در تحت تقدیرات و خواست ما منکوب و ذلیل و خوار و ضعیف است. اینست که اسم او را در بارگاه ما هم به شوکت و احترام ذکر کردی.

"My God, it's out of fear and apprehension regarding the aforementioned facts."

"Take this Sheykh away, there's no time to lose." They took him and placed him in the pre-ordained place.

The Herald called out: "Mirzâ Mohammad Hâshem Chahârsuqi."[64] The chamberlains of heavenly power brought him to the scales of justice. Once again I was seized by an extraordinary anxiety to know what they would do to this man. We considered him to be one of the saints who are near to God. If all the people did not confirm this, the position of that poor man would have been too terrible to tell. Oh Oh Oh!

I was reflecting on these things when an angel approached and gave me a dig in the ribs, saying, "Don't concern yourself with what has occurred or will occur in the affairs of God. Be all eyes and ears, to see what there is to see and hear." These words had a strange effect on me. I immediately became like a statue, eyes wide open and ears straining.

The Voice said, "Mohammad Hashim, given the divine favours we bestowed on you, what acts of thankfulness have you rendered to us, what benevolence have you shown to our Muslim faithful?"

"Well, there's this and that. There's the burden of age, and… and…" Then he called on everyone to shout 'salavat' in unison.[65]

"Seyyed, you're not in a hospital! This is the place of reward and punishment. Even the prophets must come here, powerless and supplicating, to pay their debts penny for penny and grain for grain!"

"Just so. I'm sufficiently well educated to know that. I've read a lot about the practicalities and particularities of the Place of Assembly." He turned to the assembly and said, "Raise a loud salavat!"

The Voice spoke to the angels on his right and left, saying,

جواب: الهی از خوف و وحشت ملاحظه‌های مذکوره.
خطاب: ببرید شیخ را که بیش از این مجال نیست. بردند و در مقام معهود مقیمش نمودند.
منادی ندا درداد: میرزا هاشم چهارسوقی.
فراشان قدرت الهی او را در محل میزان حساب حاضر نمودند باز اضطراب فوق العاده مرا فرا گرفت که آیا با این شخص دیگر چه کنند آنکه ما او را در رتبهٔ یکی از اولیای مقرب می‌دانستیم چنان شد و اگر یک تصدیق عامه نبود بیچاره نمیدانم در چه شداید بود ایشان! که وای وای وای.
در این خیال بودم که ملکی نزدیک شده لطمه به من زده گفت: در امورات الهی، چه شد چه میشود مکن، تمام چشم باش تا چه بینی و گوش باش تا چه شنوی. گویا این حرف اثر غریبی در من کرد که فوراً به همان حالت مجسمه‌وار چشم را خیره و گوش را تیز کرده ایستادم.
خطاب: محمد هاشم از نعمتهای الهی که به تو دادیم چه شکرانه و خوشنودی برای ما و مسلمانان ما آوردی؟
جواب: بلی، چنین و چنان. کسالت پیری و، و، و، یک صلوات بلندی ختم کنید.
خطاب: آقا سید اینجا مریض خانه نیست. اینجا مقام مجازات و مؤاخذات است. اینجا پیغمبران با حالت عجز و لابه باید حساب خود را ذره ذره و ارزن ارزن بپردازند.
جواب: چنین، این قدرها سواد داریم که بدانیم اعمال و تفصیلات محشر را، خیلی خوانده‌ایم، چنین، یک صلوات بلندی ختم کنید.
خطاب شد به ملک یمین و یسار او که:

"The things this man is saying hold no water. You, who are responsible for his good and bad deeds, take bodily form beside him and show his character and deeds to him."

Two angels appeared beside him. The one on his left was very sturdily built, fearsome and black. No pen could describe how fearsome he was. The angel on his right was well proportioned and pleasing of face. It was as if, through the appearance of these two angels, one beautiful and the other hideous, all the deeds of that gentleman had become visible to all those assembled there.

To the angel who recorded the Seyyed's misdeeds, the Voice said, "Do not show the scroll that records his deeds; conceal it from the eyes of the residents of the Place of Assembly, because if they see it, we too would be indignant and ashamed."

The man turned to the angel and said: "There is no god but God. I never thought I was so bad."

The Voice said: "You pronounce the sentiments of divine unity, but you did not perform the deeds of unity."

"Surely I did," he said, "I have even read the Koran."

"Yes, *They read the Koran, saying with their lips what was not in their hearts.*"[66]

Then the voice summoned the recorder of that gentleman's sins: "Have you observed, during all this time, any ruling or judgement that this man has issued in accordance with justice and the rules of religious law?"

"Hardly," came the answer.

"His knowledge of religious law and principles was, in comparison to the other ulama of Isfahan, large," the Voice observed. "Why were his rulings so unsound?"

"Because he had less faith," the angel answered.

"How many of the Muslims' riches, estates and rights have been confiscated and plundered by certain tormentors, by gaining possession of the signature and seal of this Seyyed?"

The angel said, "O my God, there were certain people who

مذاکرات آقا گویا از روی مأخذی نیست. شما را که موکلین اعمال زشت و خوب نموده‌ایم در طرفینش مجسم شوید و تشریح حال و اعمال او بنمائید.

دو ملک که یکی خیلی قوی الجثه و مهیب و سیاه رنگ بود که ذکر هیبت او بتحریر نمی‌آید در طرف چپ و ملک دیگر که نیکواندام و خوبرو بود در طرف راست جناب آقا حاضر شده و گوئی از ظهور این دو ملک حسن و قبح تمام اعمال آقا بر همه اهل محشر مکشوف گردید.

به ملک کاتب سیئات مشارالیه خطاب رسید که:

طومار ثبت اعمال آقا را ارائه مکن و مخفی دار که اهالی محشر مشاهده ننمایند. زیرا از ملاحظه آن ما خود نیز رنجش و خجلت حاصل می‌نمائیم.

آقا رو به ملک مذبور کرده، فرمودند:

لا اله الا الله چنین گمان سوئی را نمی‌کردم.

خطاب رسید: کلمهٔ توحید می‌گوئی و حال آنکه اعمال آنرا رفتار ننموده‌ای.

آقا عرض کردند: بلی یقولون بافواههم ما لیس فی قلوبهم.

بعد به کاتب سیئات آقا ندا رسید که: آیا در این مدت حکم و قضاوتی را دیده‌ای که آقا به عدالت و قانون شریعت بنماید؟

عرض کرد: کمتر.

خطاب رسید: علم و فقه و اصولش که نسبتاً بیشتر از سایر علمای اصفهان بود آیا جهت بی استحکامی احکامش چه بود؟

عرض کرد: به عوض اعتقاداتش کمتر بود.

خطاب: چه بسیار املاک و اراضی و حقوق مسلمانان را که بعضی تعدی کنندگان به استمساک امضاء و مهر این سید ضبط و غصب کرده‌اند.

عرض: الهی چندین نفر بودند که

counterfeited the seal and signature of this gentleman, and when they returned to him with some other trickery, he was forced to confirm their validity and authority."

"Have you recorded all this?"

"My God, you are the One who knows what is concealed. What power do we have to deviate from your command? You gave the order to conceal, and you have shown mercy to spare your servant from shame and confusion."

"Did you register the names and particulars of these people, who imitated his signature and his stamp?"

His Eminence (Mirzâ Mohammad Hâshem Chahârsuqi) turned to the angel who recorded his sins and said, with great indignation and asperity, "It's clear that you, like the clergy of the Royal Mosque (meaning, Âqâ Najafi, Âqâ Hâjji Sheykh Mohammad-'Ali and Hâjji Âqâ Nurollâh), are making allegations about me. Did more than two persons counterfeit my seal and forge contracts? The first was Asadollâh Khadije Farangi, the second was Seyyed Taqi Mâzanderâni. And they didn't stop with imitating my seal and signature! They counterfeited the seal and signature of anyone they pleased. That's how it was, but doesn't God know this himself? Let us raise a salavat."

The angel for sins said: "Good sir, you knew only these two, but you knew what sort of people they were. Because they carried out their duties, you closed your eyes. But we know some others."

That gentleman said, "You are not worthy to ascribe such things to the ulama. An ignorant man does not dispute with a religious scholar."

The holy Voice spoke: "This Seyyed has become very old. '*It is not a blame on the sick.*' (24: 61) Bring the other ulama."

When the names of the other ulama were read, I saw about three hundred to four hundred of the great gentry brought together from among the throng of strangers. The Voice said: "Isfahan did not have so many theologians and ulama. We have reviewed their accounts up to the time of Hajji Sheykh Mohammad Baqer, and we have given each the appropriate recompense. What is going on

مهر و امضاء این آقا را می‌ساختند و بعد دوباره به تدلیس دیگر نزد خودش آورده صحت و اعتبارش را مجبور به نوشتن می‌شد.
خطاب: همه را در ثبت داری؟
عرض: بارالها تو خود عالم‌الغیوبی چگونه در ماموریت خود ما قدرت مخالفت داریم. آنست که امر فرمودی مخفی دار و ترحم نمودی که این بنده عاصیت خجل و شرمسار نشود.
خطاب: اسم و رسم اشخاصی هم که امضاء و مهر او را ساختند ثبت داری؟
جناب آقا با کمال تغیر و خشونت رو کرد به ملک کاتب سیئات و گفت: معلوم می‌شود تو هم مثل بچه مسجد شاهی ها (مقصود آقا نجفی، آقای شیخ محمد علی و حاجی آقا نورالله است) با من مدعی هستی. مگر اشخاصی که مهر مرا می‌ساختند و ند و قبالهٔ ساختگی درست می‌کردند دو نفر بیشتر بودند. اول اسداله خدیجه فرنگی، دوم سید تقی مازندرانی. اینها هم که منحصر به مهر و امضای من نبود، مهر و امضای همه کس را می‌ساختند.
چنین، مگر خدا خودش نمی‌داند، یک صلوات بلند ختم کنید.
ملک سیئات: جناب آقا شما این دو نفر را بیشتر نمی‌شناختید و می‌دانستید که حالشان چیست و چون به وظیفهٔ خود عمل می‌کردند شما اغماض می‌نمودید. ما بعضی دیگر را می‌شناسیم.
جناب آقا: شما را نمی‌رسد که نسبت به علما این جوابات را بدهید. جاهل را بر عالم بحثی نیست.
خطاب مستطاب رسید: این سید خیلی سنش زیاد شده. لیس علی المریض حرج. سایر علما را بیاورید.
اسم سایر (علما) که برده شد قریب سیصد و چهارصد نفر از آقایان عظام را دیدم که ازدحام غریبی فراهم آوردند.
خطاب رسید که: اصفهان اینقدر مجتهد و عالم نداشت ما تا قبل از حاجی شیخ محمد باقر را به حسابشان رسیده هر یک را به اندازهٔ خود هر چه لایق بوده‌اند جزا داده‌ایم. چه خبر است

here? How were all these gentlemen and theologians gathered in such a short time? O Gabriel, make enquiries and inform the court."

Gabriel answered, "My God, each of these people considers himself to rank as a 'Proof of Islam.'[67] You would not even consider them capable of interpreting scripture, which makes your instruction to examine them more urgent."

However, the command to investigate [was repeated], even more urgently. Gabriel conveyed the command of the Lord of Lords to the notables and to the crowd. Full of pride and conceit, they all deposited their turbans and outer robes in the garderobe, drew out their writing cases and affirmed for one another that they were all Proofs of God, and presented this in answer to Gabriel.

The Voice said, "O Gabriel! Lately, and especially in Isfahan, reasoning from scripture and the leadership of the religious community is nothing more than the size of one's turban and speaking with gutturals.[68] But clothes don't make the man.[69] Learning and effort have been abolished. Quite simply, each one of them who wanted to be more a Proof of Islam [than the others] would take a pilgrimage to the shrines in Iraq, to Holy Najaf. And that's enough. Tell this group that we will require each of them to sit a test of knowledge. Each of them who is not qualified to be a theologian or ulama will be severely punished, and subject to our extreme anger."

This summon and its expression were so accusatory and wrathful that the earth in the place of the assembly began to shake and a strange boundless perturbation seized the whole gathering, particularly this group of fraudulent ulama. After this, each of these mullahs lowered his head in shame and rejoined his own community. One group joined the gathering of rustics from around Isfahan, a few joined the footmen and gatekeepers, and one group joined the workers and clerks. In this way, they gradually dispersed, little by little, until very few of them remained. When I looked carefully again, I could not see any one of those gentlemen before the scales

و در این مدت کم این همه آقایان و مجتهدین چگونه فراهم آمده‌اند؟ یا جبرئیل تحقیق کن و به درگاه ما خبرش را بیاور.

جبرئیل عرض کرد: الهی هر یک از اینها خود را حجت الاسلام می‌دانند، شما به اجتهاد هم قبولشان نمی‌فرمائید. مسئله غامض تر شد و امر به تحقیق اکیدتر گردید. جبرئیل امر حضرت رب الارباب را به حضرات و جمعیت رسانید. با کمال غرور و نهایت تکبر هر یک عمامه و عبای خود را با نعلین ترتیب داده و قلمدانها را کشیده همگی حجت الاسلامی یکدیگر را تصدیق نمودند و به حضرت جبرئیل عرض عریضه داشتند.

خطاب رسید: یا جبرئیل در این اوان و در این دوران خصوصاً در اصفهان اجتهاد و ریاست ملیه جز به بزرگی عمامه و غلیظ حرف زدن و عمامه دست ژولیده و یک نعلین پوست خربزه بیش نیست علم و زحمت و فضل منسوخ شده منتهی هرکدام که می‌خواستند خیلی حجت الاسلام تر باشند یک سفر عتبات یا نجف اشرف امر را کامل می‌دارد، به این گروه بگو که ما یکی یک شما را در مقابل امتحان علمیه خواهیم آورد و هر کدام لیاقت اجتهاد و عالمیت را نداشته باشید به اشد عذاب و نهایت غضب ما گرفتار خواهید شد.

این ندا و خطاب به قسمی عتاب و غضب امیز بود که زمین محشر به لرزه در آمد و اضطراب غریبی هر یک از جمعیت نامتناهی را دست داد خصوصاً این جمعیت علمای مصنوعی را! و بعد از آن هر یک سر خجلت پائین انداخته به طائفه خود ملحق شدند، جمعی به حوزهٔ رعایای اطراف اصفهان، برخی به فراشان و نوکربابان، گروهی به کارگران و عمله جات و ناوه کشان ــ کم کم به این طریق گم شدند تا عدهٔ خیلی قلیلی باقی مانده. بعد از آن خوب نگریستم کسی را در پای میزان حساب از آقایان

of justice. Each of them, based on their own work, had returned to his natural place. A torrent of laughter and exclamations of great astonishment swept over the onlookers.

Then came the summons, "Bring in Sheykh Mohammad Taqi, the son of Sheykh Mohammad Bâqer."

The chamberlains of heavenly power brought him before the scales of justice. The Voice said, "Mohanmad Taqi, have you ever reflected on this day, have you ever given a single thought to this Court and its punishments?"

"I do not know what is hidden," he replied, "can he?" (Sheykh Mohammad Taqi's responses should be read with an Esfahani accent.)

"O Sheykh, don't start here, with the sort of answers you gave to the ignorant on earth! Methinks summoning you another time has made you doubt whether your knowledge and qualification really justified a position of leadership on earth. Make no mistake, this summons is purely a calling to account, to see why you did not demonstrate the deeds and requisites of [leadership]."

"I? I had no leadership at all. These oppressors had leadership, these madmen, these... these..."

"When we address you and call you to account, you should answer clearly and correctly. This of all places is no place for the worldly dissimulation and neglect of religion you have been accustomed to use in your own interests. Explain yourself! Here you are addressing the court of Unicity and Divinity, not the street sweepers and fools of Isfahan, who gave their allegiance to you through a manifest deceit. To wink and be negligent is customary among such people, but not here."

When Sheykh Taqi saw the signs of wrath and severity, he fell to imploring and confessing his weakness, "Taqi is only a poor weak creature. Everything you say, he has accepted. What should he do now?"

"Mohammad Taqi," said the Voice, "do you remember the time when you desired to have an entire village without any problems involved?

ندیدم. هر یک پی کار خود رفته و به اصل خود رجوع نموده بودند. این دفعه قهقهه و تعجب عظیمی از نظاره کنندگان برخاست.

ندا رسید: شیخ محمد تقی پس شیخ محمد باقر را حاضر نمائید. فراشان قدرت در پای میزان حساب حاضرش ساختند.

خطاب رسید: محمد تقی امروز را هیچ تصور میکردی و این محکمه و مؤاخذات را آیا به خاطر خطور میدادی؟

جواب: من که غیب نمی‌دونم (جوابهای شیخ محمد تقی را می باید با لهجۀ اصفهانی خواند) او چه طور؟

خطاب: یا شیخ، جواب هائی را که در دنیا به تجاهل میدادی اینجا شروع مکن. گویا احضار ثانوی تو را به شک انداخته که شاید به علم و استحقاق در دنیا ریاست داشته ای، اشتباه مکن که این احضار محض مؤاخذات است که چرا به اعمال و لوازم آن رفتار ننمودی.

جواب: منکه ریاستی نداشتم ریاست را این ظلمه، این دیوونیا اینا اینا...

خطاب: مؤاخذات و خطابات ما را میبایست جواب متین و صحیح داد، این مقام مقامی نیست که تدلیسات و تجاهلهای دنیا را که یکی از پیشرفت امور خود دانسته بودی بیان نمائی. اینجا با بارگاه احدیت و الوهیت گفتگو میکنی نه با کودکان و احمقان اصفهان که به گول اظهار ارادت به تو میکردند. غمض و تجاهل کردن با آنان عادت این مقامت نشود.

چون علامت غضب و سختی را مشاهده کرد به عجز و لابه عرض کرد.

جواب: تقی که بندۀ ضعیف بیچاره‌ای بیش نیست هر چه شوما بفرمائید حاضرس، حالا باید چی کار کرد؟

خطاب: محمد تقی آیا زمانی را بخاطر داری که آرزوی یک ده ششدانگی بی دردسر می کردی. چه گریه ها. چه لابه ها می‌نمودی بدرگاه ما،

What tears you wept, how you implored our Court! After each of our favours you wept and pleaded and there was no end of it, until your endless petitions moved our mercy. We answered your prayers, just to end the matter. We bestowed on you the ownership or part ownership of towns and villages, and made their resources available so that you could dispose of any property as you saw fit. First you became a land-owner, a rich man, a planter and a power to be reckoned with; we require an acknowledgement from you. How liberally have we bestowed on you our mercy and bounties?"

"It's true," he replied, "but you gave these benefits yourself, I thought we had a deal! How have I wronged you?"

"Sheykh Taqi, did we create you without modesty and shame, that you give such answers in the presence of our Oneness?"

"According to the religious law," he replied, "an accusation must be made convincing, that is, corroborated, to the extent that dubious things are clarified."

"O Sheykh Taqi! This place is the Fountain-head of Glory. Here, in our judgement and chastisement, there is no distinction between the prophets and messengers of God and the least of our creatures. Now, finally, tell us: what deeds of service have you done in exchange for our manifold bounties? Have we not entrusted you, outwardly, with our religious law? What service did you perform for the people of Islam? What charitable foundations have you established? In sum, except for thinking about fixing prices and hoarding grain, and increasing the scope of your own estates, what deeds have you done? What religious devotions have you performed? How have you suffered for the well-being of the people, what have you sacrificed for the well-being of the poor? What efforts have you made for the progress of the sciences of the Islamic world?"

"I have promulgated Islamic law," he said. "But have you not been informed that several times, certain people of Isfahan wanted to build a school, but they wanted to gather children there and teach them in an outlandish way. They said that after six months, the children would read the Koran well and write well.

بعد از هر فریضه اشکها میریختی التماس ها می کردی و میسرت نمی‌شد تا تضرعات بی اندازهٔ تو رحمت ما را محرک شده دعایت را به موقف اجابت رسانیدیم. ده ها و قراء عدیدهٔ مشترک و مختص به تو مرحمت کردیم و اسبابش را فراهم آوردیم که هر ملکی را به عنوانی و به شکلی تصرف نمودی، اول ملاک شدی، اول دولتمند شدی، اول زارع شدی، اول با قدرت شدی، از خودت تصدیق میخواهیم. ترحم و عنایات ما چقدر خوشبختی به تو مرحمت فرمود؟

جواب: او بله اما اینا رو که خودتون داده‌اید مثل اینکه صلح کرده بودید. من او چه تقصیری دارم؟

خطاب: ای شیخ حجب و حیا در تو مگر ما خلق نکرده‌ایم که این جوابها را در مقام احدیت ما میدهی؟

جواب: شرعاً مدعی را باید مجاب کرد یا اثبات که شد اون وقت اشکال پیدا میکوند.

خطاب: ای شیخ تقی اینجا مصدر جلالت است. اینجا پیغمبران و رسل در محاکمه و مؤاخذه با ضعیف‌ترین بندهٔ ما فرقی ندارد. در عوض نعمتهای گوناگون ما آخر بگو چه خدمتی کردی؟ مگر نه شرع خود را ظاهراً به تو سپردیم چه خدمتی به ملت اسلام کردی؟ چه بنای خیری نهادی؟ تمام جز اینکه در فکر تسعیر و جمع غله بودی و وسعت املاک خود را کوشش می‌نمودی چه کاری نمودی؟ چه عبادت روحانی کردی؟ چه شدتی برای راحتی خلق و چه اذیتی برای راحتی فقرا کشیدی؟ چه همتی در ترقی علوم امت اسلام نمودی؟

جواب: ترویج شریعت کردم. مگر به شما نگفتند این چند دفعه بعضی از اهل اصفهون میخواستن مدرسه دروس به کونند، اما میخواستن اونجا بچه ها را جمع کونند یک جور غریبی درس بدند، می‌گفتند بچه ها شش ماهه قرآن خب می خوند، خط خب می نویسد،

Whatever book you gave them, they would read well. But they also said that they would teach the children a Christian language at the same time. I thought, 'this can't be!' First there would be learning a Christian language, little by little, and at the same time the children would be reading the religious law. The Islamic scholars would have to learn the blasphemous language, and that would not be good. I said they should close the place one way or the other. I even wrote ten or twenty letters to the Prince. Then it became apparent that it was just one school, no more than that. But despite what they said, I sent some people to close it. Wasn't this promulgating Islamic law?"

"Sheykh Taqi," said the Voice, "you're very good at deception and trickery. You're perfect at it, and eloquent without blushing. Satan is a mere student compared to you, for your trickery is more imaginative deception than his."

These words were not completed before Sheykh Taqi's composure was altered. With an angry and excited expression on his face, he said, "You! You scoff at the religious law. What you say is... Oh! it is not good to scoff at the knowledge of the learned... that is apostasy."

The Voice spoke: "Sheykh Taqi, even if you believe that Omar usurped the caliphate, you have to admit how much he contributed to Islam. He conquered several cities, and he promulgated Islam in the political affairs of his day. You have hindered the progress of the religious community. You have scattered a gathering of those who were engaging in teaching and rearing Muslim children. You have rendered the schools that educated my children barren, and now you make it your boast! 'Oh I'm the one who caused ignorance, I'm the one who closed the school for Muslim children.' Are you unable to blush? We read the heart of every individual. We know that it is you who prevented the people from setting up schools, and you put bounds on the pursuit of scientific studies, because their incomprehension and ignorance sustained your power and leadership. You regarded the promulgation of the religious law as a way of furthering your own interests. Whenever someone mocked you personally or your ideas, something would happen. Either you

او دیگه هر کتابی یم که بدند بچه خب می خوند. اما می گفتند می خواند این بچه ها زبونی نصاری هم باز بوخونند. من دیدم که خوب نمی‌شد آ اونوقت زبونی نصاری کم کم یاد می گیرند و اونوقت بچه ها سواد هم کو دارند شریعت علماء اسلام زبونی کفر شاید یاد می‌گیرند او خب نبود، گفتم هر طور بود رفتند او اونجا را بستند. ده بیست کاغذ به شازده هم نوشتم، بعد معلوم شد که همین یک مکتبی بوده چیزی دیگه نبود. اما محض اینکه این چیز ها را گفتند فرستادم بستند او این ترویج شریعت نبود؟

خطاب: شیخ تقی خیلی در تدلیس و تجاهل دست کامل داری و بی خجالت زبان آوری می‌نمائی ابلیس باید نزد تو شاگرد شود که مدلس تر از آنی و هم مزورتر.

هنوز این خطاب تمام نشده که حالت آقا متغیر شده با چهرهٔ تعرض انگیزی گفت: او شوما که تو هین شریعت میکونید این حرفهای شوما... او چرا خوب نیست توهین عالم عالم ... که مرتد بود.

خطاب آمد: شیخ تقی اگر به عقیدهٔ تو (عمر غصب خلافت) کرد در نگاهداری بیضه اسلام هم چقدر کوشش نمود چندین شهر را فتح کرد. امور سیاسی آن زمان را در اسلام چقدر ترویج داد. تو مانع ترقی ملت شدی مجمعی که در صدد تعلیم و آموزش اطفال مسلمانان بوده‌اند، بر هم زدی. مدرس و مکتب تحصیل اطفال بندگان مرا بایر کردی، و اکنون افتخار می کنی منم که باعث بی علمی شدهام، منم که مدرسه دائرهٔ اطفال مسلمانان را بستهام و خجالت نمی‌کشی؟ ما از درون هر نفسی آگاهیم و میدانیم که تو مردم را منع از افتتاح مدارس و تحصیلات علوم عهد می‌نمودی که نافهم و بی علم باشند تا تو به اقتدار و ریاست خود باقی بمانی. تو ترویج شریعت را ترویج شخصی خودت می دانستی، هر وقت توهین شخصی یا بر ضد خیال نفسانیت اتفاقی پیش می‌افتاده

would accuse them of being a Bâbi and command their execution, or you had the poor fellow flogged for drinking wine, or you would threaten someone, merely to satisfy your own delusions, by saying this is perverting the principles of Islam. Or if it was reported that things contrary to the religious law had taken place in any house, you would block the door of the house with clay."

Meanwhile, in the midst of the crowd, I saw a commotion beginning. There were cries of "Oh, the villain, oh, the villain! Curses on you. Curses on you." I looked more closely, and saw Haji Heyder-'Ali, who held in his hands several tambourines, stringed instruments and a violin. He was accompanied by several men, two or three women and other people. He was breathless, but when his eyes fell on his Eminence Najafi, he said, "Sir, I was going down one of the streets of Isfahan when I heard the sound of music, dancing and song in the house of this rascal. Thinking of you, I summoned several students of theology. We broke the door and entered the house, and we saw these wretches singing and dancing, which is contrary to the venerable law of Islam. After punishing them thoroughly and giving them a good beating, they said they were celebrating a wedding. These rascals, may they be cursed, quickly dropped their instruments and broke them. What a hubbub!"

His Eminence filled with pride, he cast a withering glance at the fountainhead of divine power, as if to say to God, 'See the result of my promulgation of Islamic law and my appointing people to preserve Islamic laws.' The poor residents of that house, men and women, were so ashamed and in such a state that words cannot describe it.

The voice of reproach was heard from the fountainhead of power, saying, "Bravo! Bravo Sheykh. It has become clear to me how you protect Islamic law. Where, in Islamic law, is it said that one may enter a house without permission, or violate so flagrantly the respect and honour of Muslims? Does not the law of Mohammad, peace be upon him, command emphatically and explicitly that one may not enter any

یک کسی را به تهمت بابیگری! حکم قتل می دادی بیچاره را به عنوان شرب خمر حد می زدی یا شخصی را محض اجرای خیال خود به فساد عقیده تهدید می کردی یا خانه‌ئی را با شعار وقوع خلاف شرع درب آن را گل میگرفتی.
در این ضمن در بحبوحهٔ ازدحام دیدم شلوغ و غوغائی بر پا شد. فریادهای: ای خبیث ای خبیث و فریادهای: ای ملعون، ای ملعون به گوش رسید. خوب ملتفت شدم دیدم حاجی حیدر علی چند دائره و تار و کمانچه و سه تار در دست گرفته، چند مرد و دو سه زن را با سایر همراهان خود جلو کرده می‌آیند. چشمش به جناب مستطاب آقا نجفی افتاد هن هن کنان و حس حس زنان گفت: آقا در یکی از کوچه های اصفهان عبور میکردم از خانه این خبیث (رو کرد به مرد صاحبخانه) دیدم صدای تغنی و سماع و آواز و ساز می‌آید. از قول آقا بعضی طلاب خبر کردم ریختیم درب خانه را شکستیم. داخل شدیم دیدیم این خبیث‌ها مشغول ترنم و این خلاف شرع عظیم هستند پس از اینکه ایشان را خوب تنبیه کردیم و کتک شدید زدیم میگویند عروسی داشتیم. خبیث‌ها ملعون ها فوراً دائره ها و آن اسبابها را بنا کردند به زمین زدن و خورد کردن ترق و تروق عظیمی از شکستن آن آلات استماع شد.
جناب آقا بادی زیر بغل خود انداخته نظری حقیرانه به سمت مصدر جلال الهی نموده که معلوم میداشت میفرمایند:"مشاهدهٔ این ترویجات شریعت و استخدام گماشتگان مرا در حفظ حدود اسلام بنمائید. بیچاره اهل آن خانه زنانه و مردانه چه خجالتها بردند و چه حالتی داشتند نمیتوانم بیان نمایم.
خطاب عتاب انگیز از مصدر جلال رسید که: به به واقعاً تشرع تو ای شیخ معلوم شد و مکشوف گردید. کجا شریعت اسلام حکم می کند که بی اذن داخل خانه شوی یا عرض و ناموس مسلمانی را به این اصرار به باد دهی؟ مگر نه در شریعت محمد (ص) امر اکید و اصرار بلیغ شده که بی اذن داخل منزل کسی نشوید

house without permission, even when the door is open? Is not this the literal and clear text of the book of God? Isn't the protection of the respect and honour of the Muslims confirmed to such an extent in the Islamic law? Have we not forbidden you from scrutinizing and examining the opinions of Muslims? Have we not given explicit orders to consider the acts of Muslims with a sympathetic eye? And finally, why did you imagine that their behaviour was simply for the pleasure of music? You've jumped to conclusions before they had spoken. You claim to be a qualified mujtahid. Why do you entrust judgement to the least of your servants? They ascertained the facts and implemented the punishment themselves. Bravo, Bravo! But what if they were enjoying music on the basis of Islamic law? For example, with certain diseases, we have created no remedy except for music and dance. Perhaps it was done on the orders of a doctor? If we consider your errors and misdeeds under Islamic law in this matter, then your punishment will be a hundred times harder."

The Sheykh said: "No, no, Haji Heyder-'Ali tells the truth and is just in his acts! Don't imagine such things of him."

"O trustees of heaven!" thundered the Voice, "punish the guilty!"

A number of angels came with incandescent chains and fiery spears. The poor Haji Heyder-'Ali ran to that gentleman and clung to his robe, pleading, "Sir, Sir, protect me! O Sir, see what a calamity has descended upon me. O Sir, woe is me! Sir, do something! I'm not to blame. Sir, you ordered me to do it yourself."

As was his habit, that Eminence stroked his beard and held his head high, and looked down on Heyder-'Ali, and with a calm, soft voice, he said, "It's no longer my duty to concern myself with your affairs. Go now, I'll see you later."

They took poor Haji Heyder-'Ali, who for the sake of earning a crust of bread had sacrificed himself to the court of the Sheykh, and was now entangled in everlasting punishment. They entrusted him and those with him to the guardians of hell. What they did to them, and how extreme their punishment was, God alone knows.

ولو درب منزل باز هم باشد؟
مگر نه نص صریح کتاب الله است. مگر نه حفظ ناموس و آبروی مسلمانان تا چه درجه در شرع اسلام تاکید شده؟
مگر نه امر کرده‌ایم که تجسس و تعمق در عقاید مسلمانان نکنید؟
مگر نه حکم مؤکد نموده‌ایم که اعمال مسلمانان را حمل به خیر نمائید؟
آخر از کجا معلوم شد که حرکت ایشان فقط محض تغنی بوده. هنوز به تو نگفته ثابت گردید. تو خود ادعای اجتهاد میکنی، ادنی نوکرانت چرا اجرای احکام می‌کنند. به خود آنها ثابت شد و کیفر هم دادند. به به و حال آنکه شاید به علت شرعی مشغول تغنی بوده‌اند چنانچه در بعضی امراض معالجه‌ای جز تغنی و سماع ما خلق نکرده‌ایم شاید به دستور حکیمی بوده اگر خلاف و خطای شرعی بوده که از تو در همین رفتار صادر شده بیان نمائیم کیفر تو صد چندان می‌شود.
آقا فرمودند: خیر خیر حاجی حیدرعلی موثق و جزوی عدولس (عادل است). شما بعضی خیالات در حقش نکونید.
خطاب: ای خازنین درکات مرتکبین را بسزای خود برسانید.
ریختند ملائکه چندی با زنجیرهای آتشین و عمودهای مشتعل. بیچاره حاجی حیدرعلی دوید دست به دامن آقا شد ای آقا دخیلم امان ای آقا ببین چه بلیه بسر دارم اقا وای وای وای وای ای اقا کاری بکن که این گه ها را نمیخوردم ای اقا تو خودت دستورالعمل دادی جناب آقای نجفی به عادت معهود و حالت محدود دستی به زیر و بالای ریش کشیده گردن را بالا گرفته چشمها را به چشم حاجی حیدرعلی انداخته با صدائی آهسته و ملایم فرمودند: دیگر تکلیف شرعی من نیست در کار شوما دخالت کونم حالا شوما تشریف ببرید بعد دیگر شوما را ملاقات خواهم کرد.
بیچاره حاجی حیدرعلی را که محض کسب لقمه نانی خود را فدائی درگاه آقا کرده بود و به این خطر و انتقام ابدی خود را گرفتار نمود- بردند با تابعین و همراهانش به مالک دوزخ سپردند. آیا با او چه کردند خدا داناست. آیا با چه شدائید به او کیفر دادند.

When that gentleman observed this commotion, he became visibly anxious. He had been pondering what had been discussed, and his answers became less obtuse.

"O Sheykh," said the Voice, "did you not know that the development of any nation depends on its knowledge and sciences?"

"Yes," he replied.

"Did you not see how sciences were spreading in other countries, and how progress depends on them?"

"Yes."

"Do you not understand that the strength of other countries, as compared to the abject state of the Iranian people, is due to the dissemination of the sciences, and the opening of schools, which they have undertaken and promoted, while you have opposed and restricted them?"

"Yes."

"Then why did you prevent with such tenacity the opening of schools and the spread of sciences? Are you opposed to the progress of the people?"

"We have several schools in Isfahan. The School of Chahâr Bâgh, the School of Nim Avard Kaseh Garan, the School of Mulla 'Abdolah, and so on and so forth. In all these schools the students are taught sciences. That's the truth."

"Sheykh," said the Voice, "do you pretend ignorance? What do they teach in these schools? Do they teach arithmetic, geography, mathematics, practical knowledge, political science and the like, which are the most useful sciences?"

"They teach religious jurisprudence, the fundaments of theology, and exegesis."

"O Sheykh! To know religious jurisprudence is to know codified law, which other countries print and publish in a language the common people understand. They sell it in the bazaar and in the alleyways. Every old woman and every child knows it, while you encumber the systematic law of the Prophet Mohammad, which is the most sufficient of all codes of

جناب آقا این هنگامه را که ملاحظه فرمودند چه حالت اضطرابی برایشان پیدا شد. قدری در مکالمات ملاحظات داشتند و جواب جهالت آمیز کمتر می دادند.
خطاب رسید: ای شیخ مگر نمی دانستی که ترقی هر ملتی به علم و دانش است؟
جواب: چرا.
خطاب: مگر نمی دیدی که انتشار علوم در ملل سایره تا به چه درجه و ترقی هر ملتی به علم و دانش است؟
جواب: چرا.
خطاب: مگر نمی فهمیدی که اقتدار سایر ملل و ذلت ملت ایران به علت انتشار و افتتاح مدارس است که آنها اقدام کرده و انبساط داده‌اند و شما اغماض نموده و انقباض کرده‌اید.
جواب: چرا.
خطاب: پس چرا به این اصرار مانع افتتاح مدارس و علوم شده مخل ترقی مردم شدی؟
جواب: مدارس عدیده در اصفهون داریم مدرسۀ چهارباغ، مدرسۀ نیم آورد کاسه گران، مدرسه ملا عبدالله و غیره و غیره... در تمام این مدارس طلاب عموم کار میکنند اینها همه هست.
خطاب: یا شیخ باز تجاهل کردی؟ در این مدارس کدام علم تحصیل می شود؟ علوم حساب، جغرافی، ریاضی، معرفت الاشیاء، سیاسی و غیره... هیچ تدریس می‌شود که بکارترین علوم است؟
جواب: فقه و اصول و علم اجتهاد است که می آموزند.
خطاب: ای شیخ علم فقه علم قانون است که سایر ملل به زبان عوام فهم چاپ و منتشر کرده در هر سر بازار و کوچه به فروش میرسانند و هر پیرزن و بچه آگاه است و شما این قانون محمد بن عبدالله را که کافی ترین

law, with difficult words and expressions – you call it religious jurisprudence and the absolute knowledge, but in it, each refers to his own reasoning and opinions. You do whatever may be in your own personal interests and you imagine that you are acting in accordance with the sanctified Law of the Prophet or implementing the commands of God. Alas, you have not learned this codified law properly and thoroughly; rather, you have proclaimed calumnies and led my servants to their ruin."

"My God," he replied, "the government should take care of these matters, we ulama do not consider it our religious duty to take the lead in these activities."

"But when the government decided on sound and orderly customs duties, you objected. What provocation! What incitement! What urgent letters and telegrams! Finally – it's a wonder you are not ashamed – you saw yourself that the principles that had been determined were soundly based, they put Iran's domestic market on a steady basis, and yielded profits, even for the government."

"But the government officials, according to Islamic law, were not entitled in principle to do it. We acted in accordance with our religious duty."

"If all of you had behaved in accordance with your real religious duties," said the Voice, "you would not see the people of Iran in such a ruinous condition. Did you consider that it was a duty implicit in your fleeting leadership to oppose the laws and actions of your own government and to protest? You did not permit the government to take adequate measures for the progress of your own people. You kept the people stupid, uncomprehending and uneducated, so they could not take action for their own progress and you, riding on their backs, could make them suffer to achieve your own ends.

"How could you regard it as your religious duty to get an inventory of affairs from every helpless citizen who came to you for protection from oppression by government officers, saying 'we will protect your property,' and then to confiscate it yourself! How could you regard it as your religious duty to hoard loads and loads

قوانین است به الفاظی و عباراتی مشکل درآورده اسمش را فقه و علم مطلق می نامید و در آن هم هریک رجوع به رأی و فتوای خود کرده هرکاری که مقصود شخصی خودتان باشد می کنید و خیال می‌کنید به شرع مطهر پیغمبر رفتار و یا به احکام حق عمل می‌کنید افسوس که این قانون را هم خوب و مستحکم نیاموخته به کذب ادعا می کنید و بندگان مرا به ضلالت می اندازید.

جواب: الهی دولت باید اینکارها را بوکوند ما علما تکلیف شرعی خود را نیدونیم در این کارها اقدام کونیم.

خطاب: مگر دولت در عمل گمرکات قانون صحیح و نظم محکم نخواست بدهد که شما چه اخلافات کردید و چه تحریکات نمودید، چه مکاتیب پرانی و تلگرافات کردید. بالاخره خودتان عجب است که خجلت نمی کشید. دیدید چه اصول صحیح و قرار محکمی بود برای تجار داخله ایران باعث رفاهیت و اسباب دخل شده دولت هم به مقصود خود نائل گردید.

جواب: دیوونیون (دیوانیان) شرعاً حق این کار را اصلاً نداشتند ماها به تکلیف شرعی خودمان رفتار کردیم.

خطاب: اگر شماها به تکلیف واقعی شرعی خود رفتار می کردید این نوع باعث ذلت ملت ایران نمی شدید. تکلیف ریاست دوروزه خود را دانسته اید که بر ضد احکام و اقدامات دولت خود رفتار نمائید و مخالفت نمایید. دولت را شما نمی گذارید برای ترقی ملت خود اقدام تامه نماید. ملت را نفهم و احمق و بی علم کرده اید که کاری پیشرفتش ننماید و شما سوارشان شده به مقصود خود به آزار آنها بکوشید.

چطور است تکلیف شرعی خود را دیدی که هر رعیت و بیچاره ای که از اجحاف عمال حکومتی به تو پناهنده شود مصالحه نامچه از او بگیری که ملکت را حفظ مینمایم و بعد ضبط نمائی. چگونه است که تکلیف شرعی خود را دیدی که گندم را انبار انبار

of wheat and, after it had rotted, to command one night that it be dumped into the river? How could you see it as your religious duty to visit the sick Mirzâ Habibollâh Khan, the Amin-al-Dowle, and then, on the pretext that he had confessed according to the religious law, to confiscate his possessions? How could you regard it as your religious duty to persuade your followers to build a dam on the river and in this way to confiscate the property of the poor?

"In what sense did you regard it as your religious duty to work hand in glove with the government to impoverish Muslims and my servants? How could you destroy them? Why did you regard it as your religious duty to buy promissory notes from the poor at a third or a quarter of their value and use them to pay taxes on your own properties? What was your motivation for sending some thugs and appropriating the property of Mirzâ Hâshem Sharafejân? What evidence did you have that your religious duty was to give the means of existence not to the Muslim poor, but rather to sturdy fat 'students' so as to fill your own classes, and increase your own self-directed power and keep the people in helpless poverty? Did you consider it your religious duty to have a new concubine every night, to go with your penis at the ready into every alleyway in Isfahan and enter the homes of all and sundry? O Sheykh, we demand the truth from you. How is a leader of the community who is so enthralled by covetous passions and power able to respond to his people's disability and impotence?"

Meanwhile, I had seen his Eminence Hâjji Âqâ Nurollâh, the brother of the aforementioned Sheykh Mohammad Taqi, known as Âqâ Najafi. Lifting his hands to the court of God, he prayed, "My God, truly, beyond doubt, behold, the world is corrupted, the world is corrupt!"

"Silence!" said the Voice. "Your turn will come."

Once again, the Voice was directed to Âqâ Najafi, saying, "O Sheykh! We have not uttered a tenth of a percent, or one gram in an ass-load, of all your detestable doings, and we are ashamed ourselves. How do you reply to what has been said?"

احتکار کنی و پس از پوسیدن، شب حکم نمائی به رودخانه بریزند؟ چطور است که تکلیف شرعی خود را در آن فهمیدی که به عیادت میرزا حبیب الله خان امین الدوله بروی و به عنوان آنکه اقرار شرعی کرده ملکش را از دست او بیرون آوردی؟ چه شده که تکلیف شرعی خود را دیدی که رعایای خود را تحریک نمائی سد و بند در رودخانه بسته املاک بیچارگان را به این حیله ضبط نمائی؟! به چه جهت تکلیف خود را دیدی که با حکومت دست یکی شده مسلمانان و بندگان مرا فقیر نموده آتش بزنی؟ علت چه بوده که تکلیف شرعی خود را دیدی که قبض مستمریات فقرا را به ثلث و ربع خریداری نمائی و به عوض مالیات املاک خود بدهی؟ سبب چه پیش آمده بود که ملک میرزا هاشم شرف جان را بفرستی عنفاً کشت و تصرف نمائی چه دلیلی داشته که تکلیف شرعی خود را دانستی که وجوهات را به فقرای اسلام نرسانی و به طلاب قوی البنیه و جثه بدهی که مدرس خود را پر جمعیت کنی و قوهٔ مقصودیهٔ خود را قوی نمائی و ملت را فقیر و بیچاره کنی؟ تکلیف شرعی خود را دانستی که هر شب دختری را صیغه و آلت خود را در دست گرفته در کوچه های اصفهان و در خانه های این و آن دخول نمائی؟

یا شیخ از خودت تصدیق می پرسیم چگونه رئیس ملتی که اینقدر هوای نفس و شهوت و مکنت دوست باشد به درد عجزهٔ ملت می تواند برسد؟ در این بین جناب حاجی آقا نورالله (برادر شیخ محمدتقی آقانجفی) را دیدم دست بدرگاه الهی بلند کرده عرض می کند الهی صدق است و شکی نیست اذا فسدالعالم فسدالعالم.

خطاب رسید: ساکت باش که نوبهٔ تو نیز خواهد رسید. مجدداً خطاب به آقای نجفی شده که:

یا شیخ- عشری از اعشار و مثقالی از خروار رفتارات قبیحه تو را نگفتم و خود شرم می آوریم در جواب این خطابات چه می گوئی؟

For a moment, the Sheykh thrust his hand under his belly and lifted it, as was his habit. For some time he scratched in his beard, and smoothed it down. Having put part of his beard into his mouth, from time to time he pulled the hairs of his own beard and parted it in two. Being busy with all this, he never gave an answer.

The Voice then spoke out in anger, "O Sheykh, what are you doing? This is not a theatre, we do not need a would-be actor."

"My God," he replied, "I believed that no-one but I knew all the things you have said. I imagined nobody at all knew what was going on. Who told you?"

"O Sheykh! Are you feigning ignorance again? What sort of nonsense is this? Respond clearly, or prepare yourself for severe penalties!"

"You should tell me who told you these details," he said, in an Isfahan dialect. "Where did you learn all this? Then I can respond. Perhaps you are friends with a foreign ambassador, or do you receive reports from the whole world like the Prince (Zell-al-Soltân)?"

"Enough of this idle talk without meaning! We know things about you that are a hundred times more excessive and uglier than this. Our patience and forgiveness do not permit you to cover yourself with disgrace and shame. We know something about you that puts even us to shame."

"These things have not been established according to Islamic law. You should better present yourself in an Islamic court to prove it or swear an oath. Otherwise, it will lead to difficulties, and my religious duty would be something different. If you say what you know, some basis – but – at least, either evidence or an oath!"

"O Sheykh! Until we have proved your misdeeds and reveal them to the people, we will not punish you. O Sheykh, we knew all that was concealed from the people. If we wanted to punish you, what a fate that would be! You would sink a thousand times deeper into the sea of ignorance and perversity, and you would suffer a hundred thousand fears in this boundless plain.

جواب: قدری به عادت مرسوم دست زیر شکم خود انداخته، شکم را بالا کشیده مقداری زیر ریش و رو را خارانیده و صاف کرده اندازهٔ موهای ریش را در دهان کرده گاهی موی ریش خود را کنده دو نیم نموده مشغول این حرکات معموله شده ابداً جوابی نمی دهد.

خطاب عتاب آمیز رسید: یا شیخ چه می کنی. اینجا بازیگرخانه و تقلیدچی لازم نیست.

جواب: بارالها من فکر میکونم اینها که شوما گفتید هیچ کس غیر از خودم نیمی دونسته خیال میکردم کسی اصلاً نمیدوند، کی به شما گفت.

خطاب: یا شیخ- باز تکرار تجاهل میکنی؟ این عنوانات احمقانه کدامست جواب صریح بازگوی- یا به شدت عذاب حاضر باش.

جواب: شوما بوگوئید این واقعات را کی به شوما گفتس او شوما فهمیدئید (لهجه اصفهانی) تا عرض کونم مگر شوما با یکی از قنسولا آشنائی دارید یا راپورت چی مثل شازده همه جای دنیا دارید؟

خطاب رسید: کم بیهوده گوئی و مهمل پرانی کن، ما اعمالی را که صد چندان از اینها اشدتر و اقبح باشد از تو دیدهایم.

اینست که اغماض و عفو ما نمی گذارد تو را به کلی رسوا و خجل نمائیم. چیزها از تو می دانیم که عنوانش اسباب انفعال ماست.

جواب: اینها که شرعاً ثابت نشده شوما خبس یا حاضر بشید در محکمهٔ شرع ثابت کونید یا قسم بخورید والا اشکال حاصل میشد و تکلیف شرعی من طوری دیگه خواهد شد او اگر بوگوئید معلوم میشد عقاید ... بل... بهرصورت یا اثبات یا قسم.

خطاب رسید: یا شیخ — ما تا خطای بنده را ثابت نکنیم به سزای آن واصلش نمی نمائیم ای شیخ تقی ما آنچه مخفی عام بوده و خود می دانستیم اگر می خواستیم مؤاخذه نمائیم وای باحوال تو که هزار بار بیش در دریای تجاهل و نادانی فرونمی رفتی و صدهزار تشویق در این صحرای نامتناهی از تغافل می کردی

O Sheykh! We grant you a favour by not punishing you for your hidden acts and not mentioning your secret intentions. But if you insist on your perversity, we will punish you for just a small part of your misdeeds, and call you to account for a drop in the ocean of your dirty secrets."

After this speech, the Sheykh became perturbed. With extraordinary anxiety, he sighed: "Truly, you are the Veiler of vices!"

The Voice said, "Suppose that we keep the extent of your behaviour in our breast, but all we have brought against you here was known to the people of Isfahan; there is nothing the people did not know. They were the talk of the street. O people of Esfahan, testify!"

At that moment, 700,000 people responded with burning cries and anguished tones that would melt the heart of a stone, or soften the heart of a tiger, "O God, we testify to what you say. We are a thousand times better informed about these things than you said. What could we do? We were just a crowd of poor people, without means and addicted to opium, caught in the strong claws of this tribe (of clerics). We could not do anything. O God, answer our plea for justice, punish those who humiliated us."

The Voice spoke: "O Sheykh! What is your answer? If you have any excuse, say it now; if you have something to add, let us hear it, because the process of proof is completed and no excuse remains."

The Sheykh tried to repeat something, using ignorance as an excuse, but his tongue and his strength failed him.

"Commit no more errors and keep the promise you gave Haji Heydar-'Ali," said the Voice. "Take him to Heydar-'Ali, so that they can meet." After this legal process and interrogation, Hâjji Sheykh Mohammad took Hâjji Âqâ Nurollâh by the hand and said, "We have seen the condition of our venerable father, and understood the punishment of our oldest brother. We cannot wait any longer. Come brother! Give me your hand and let us go to hell, as brothers." The two brothers set off in anguish.

ای شیخ ما تفضل می کنیم که اعمال مستوره ات را مؤاخذات ننموده ایم و مقاصد مکنونه ات را مذاکرات نموده ایم ولی این تجاهل و اصرار در تغافل که داری اگر تکرار نمائی جزیی از اجزای سوء رفتارت و قطره ای از دریای خبث اسرارت را بازخواست خواهیم نمود.

پس از این خطاب حالت جناب شیخ منقلب شده با اضطراب غریبی ناله کرد که یا ساترالعیوب.

خطاب رسید: گفتی مراتب رفتاراتت را ثابت داریم آنچه از تو مؤاخذات شده تمام ملت اصفهان می دانند چیزی نیست که معلوم نباشد. داستانیست که در سر هر بازاری هست. ای اهل اصفهان، شهادت خودت را بیان نمائید که یک مرتبه هفتصدهزار جمعیت با صدائی سوزناک و آوازی جگرسوز که دل سنگ را آب می نمود و جگر پلنگ را کباب، یکمرتبه عرض کردند: الهی آنچه را که خطاب فرمودی گواهیم بلکه هزار بیش از اینها آگاه. چه کنیم که یک مشت ملت فقیر بی بضاعت و عملی (تریاکی) بیش نبوده ایم و در چنگال اقتدار این طایفه کاری نمی توانستیم. بارالها تو دادخواهی ما را بکن و ذلیل کنندگان ما را به سزای خود برسان.

خطاب: یا شیخ جواب چیست؟ دیگر اگر عذری داری بیان کن و حرفی داری عنوان نما که مراتب اثبات کامل شد و عوالم اعتذار مرتفع گردید.

خواستند باز تکراری فرمایند و به تجاهل عذری دارند – زبان یارائی ننمود و قوا پایداری نکرد.

خطاب رسید: خلف مکن و به وعده ای که به حاجی حیدرعلی دادی وفا نما. ببرید در مقرا و برسانیدش تا ملاقاتی کامل حاصل نمایند.

جناب حاجی شیخ محمد علی پس از این محاکمات دست حاجی آقا نورالله را گرفت و گفت که حالت پدر بزرگوارمان را دیدیم و کیفر برادر بزرگ خود را هم فهمیدیم دیگر جای تامل نیست بیا برادر برادرانه دست همدیگر را گرفته راه دوزخ را طی نمائیم. دو برادر مأیوسانه به راه افتادند.

The Crier announced, "The love of fortune and power leads to arrogance and disregard in one's judgement of worldly and political affairs."

Hâjji Sheykh Mohammad-'Ali said, "Brother, do you hear that chilling announcement?"

Âqâ Nurollâh said, "Yes. How arrogant we have been, what ignominy we have brought upon ourselves!" So saying, the two brothers came to the mouth of hell. The licking flames of the divine wrath and vengeance made them so anxious that they were frightened and complaining beyond measure.

The Voice said, "Bring these two brothers who themselves admit to their reprehensible actions." They went themselves to the place of punishment, and were led to the scales of justice.

"What have you given us in return for the favors and graces which we have bestowed on you in this world?" the Voice continued. "What service you have rendered to the Muslims? What barriers have you raised to the cruelty of oppressors? What kind of advice did you place in the heart of the common people? How have you advanced learning? What intelligent plan did you have to advance the affairs of the Muslims? What army did you raise for the defence of Islam? What good seed have you sown to eradicate reprehensible habits? How have you increased the wealth of the people? What support did you give to the government in power? What ideas did you have for the benefit of the government and people? What consideration have you given to ensure peace and honour for the people? What efforts have you made to eliminate the poverty of the poor, or to remove the shortcomings of the weak?"

They answered, "O God, we realized what we should do at the very moment when our father and our brother were questioned here, and we went to our rightful place. Do not embarrass us further and put us to shame, because our sins are boundless, our fears beyond measure."

The Voice replied, "You do not willingly accept even one moment of hardship and anxiety.

منادی ندا درداد: حب دولت و ریاست است که در قضاوت امور و سیاست اغماض و اهمال می آورد.

حاجی شیخ محمد علی – برادر تو نیز این نوای توحش افزا را شنیدی؟

حاجی آقا نورالله- بلی چه اغماضاتی که کرده ایم چه افتضاحاتی که بکشیم. باری صحبت کنان دو برادر رسیدند نزدیک دهنۀ دوزخ. شعله های آتش غضب ربانی و زبانه های انتقام الهی چنان ایشان را به اضطراب و وحشت درآورد که بی اندازه هراسان و نالان شدند.

خطاب رسید: بیاورید این دو برادر را که خود به قبایح اعمال خود اذعان دارند و به پای خود به مقر کیفر روان شدند.

در پای میزانشان آوردند.

خطاب: شما در عوض نعمتها و عطایای ما که در دنیا متنعم بودید چه آوردید؟ چه خدمتی به نوع مسلمین کردید، چه سدی در مقابل ظلم ظالمین بستید، چه نصیحتی در قلوب عموم جا دادید، چه انتشاری در علوم نمودید؟ به چه صلاحی برای اصلاح امور مسلمانان اقدام کردید، چه سپاهی برای ثغور اسلام روانه نمودید، چه تخم خیری کاشته چه عادت زشتی را برانداختید؟ چه ثروتی برای ملت زیاد کردید، چه قوتی به دولت متبوعۀ خود دادید، چه فکری برای صولت دولت و ملت نمودید، چه کوششی در رفع فقر فقرا نمودید، چه همتی در دفع ضعف ضعفا کردید؟

جواب دادند: الهی ما در همان وقت که مؤاخذات ربانی از پدر و برادرمان می شد تکلیف خود را فهمیدیم و به منزل خود عازم شدیم. دیگر خجلت خطاب و شرم عتاب به ما مده که معاصی از حد بیرون است و اضطراب از اندازه فزون.

خطاب: یک لحظه اضطراب و سختی برای خود نمی پسندید

Think of the condition of my people, whom you kept under the continual burden of poverty, the degradation of ignorance and the suffering of lawlessness!"

Meanwhile, I saw the poet Saʻdi of Shiraz (d. 1292), who stood to one side and, in a loud voice, proclaimed:

"The sleepers do not know the suffering of those who are awake:

You will not mourn with us, unless you too know sorrow."

The Voice said, "So, you must hear the allegations about your misbehaviour, and be subject to shame and suffering, so that you may know how much bullying and wrongs you have committed. As you yourself admit, you believed that our approval depended only on obligatory prayers, fasting, the pronunciation of the Koran and pilgrimage to holy shrines. You have completely forgotten the true realities of our decrees and orders. You've ignored what we had ordered: the maintenance of prosperity, the honour of the people, the acquisition of knowledge and its perfection in practice. You have presented this in deceptive words and expressions and planted them in the hearts and minds of my helpless people. Poor traders, farmers and others, as soon as they earn a penny, or have saved some money during their lives, are all too willing and eager to spend it in holy shrines or by going to Mecca on pilgrimage, so spending all they have in another country. They return to their own country in poverty, or in debt. The poor souls are happy to have completed a pilgrimage and fulfilled their religious duty. Which of you had preached a sermon, advising these poor people that assisting and respecting the poor is a higher obligation and is better rewarded? As it is said:

'Worship is nothing more than serving people;

It does not require a rosary, a prayer mat or a coarse robe.'

Your actions and words hinder the progress of the people. They bring poverty and misery.

پس بندگان من چه حالتی داشته اند که رفتار های شما دائماً آنها را در سختی فقر و ذلت بی علمی و محنت بی قانونی انداخته بود.
در این ضمن دیدم سعدی شیرازی از گوشه ای صدا بلند کرد و بیان نمود:

خفتگان را خبر از محنت بیداران نیست
تا غمت پیش نیاید غم ما را نخوری

تمیم خطاب: پس باید به مؤاخذات سوءرفتار های خود گوش دهید و خجلت و محنت برید تا بدانید چقدر ایذا کرده اید و چه اندازه خطا نموده اید چنانچه خود اذعان دارید که می پنداشتید فقط رضایت ما به نماز و روزه با قرائت صحیح و زیارت ضریح است به کلی معانی و حقیقت احکام و اوامر ما را ترک کردید، حفظ ثروت و احترام ملت و تحصیل علم وتکمیل عمل را که واجب کرده ایم به الفاظی مخالف و عباراتی مضاد طرح کرده و در قلوب و ذهن این بندگان بیچاره من نشر دادید بینوا کسبه و رعایا و اهالی ثوسه شما که تا چهار شاهی پیدا می کنند یا عمری اگر ذخیره ای تحصیل می نمایند با کمال میل و نهایت رغبت یا در زیارت یا در خیال حج ثروت خود را به ملکی دیگر و خاکی دیگر می برند و تمام می کنند، با کمال فقر و قرض مراجعت نموده بیچاره ها دلخوش هستند که زیارت کرده ایم و تکمیل عبادت نموده ایم ولی کدام یک از شما وعظ و نصیحت به این یک مشت ملت بیچاره نموده اید که دستگیری و رعایت فقرا الزم و پراجرتر است نعم ما، قال:

عبادت به جز خدمت خلق نیست
به تسبیح و سجاده و دلق نیست

این تحریکات و حرفهای شماست که ترقی ملت را مانع می شود، فقر و پریشانی می آورد،

"According to rightful law, and the sound explanations of the Prophet and the Koran, it is clear and unmistakable that 'pilgrimage to Mecca and holy places is obligatory only when there is not a single poor, weak or hungry person among your neighbours or in your neighbourhood, or in the whole region, or even among all the Muslims or Iran.'"

The two wretched brothers threw themselves to the ground, begging and imploring, "O Lord, our sins are evident and our wrongdoings have been revealed. But we are only two of the ignorant ulama heedless doctors of religion. They too were involved and contributed to the extent of the ignorance."

The Voice said, "Our accusations are directed at people of your sort, but specific allegations have been made about individuals. The punishment of your colleagues has already been decreed and implemented. Look at the inferno and ocean of our wrath to see the penalties for such behaviour and the extent of retribution." Then it was as if a curtain had been drawn aside, or as if the barriers between the worlds had collapsed. The infinite plain of hell appeared. I looked closely at the numerous, intensely hot flames and the plains and depths of hell. Generally, I saw only eminent persons, either gentlemen or clerics, and it was apparent that, in most cases, they were in distress and the majority were tormented. Then the levels of hell returned to their original invisible condition.

The Voice said, "Have you observed that a malicious person receives his due punishment?"

The people answered, "O God, we have seen what we needed to see, and we confess our faults as we should." In the meantime, I had seen one of my oldest and closest friends, who had been away travelling for some time. I walked up to him, seized his hand and said, "My dear friend, why have you not sent a messenger or written to me during all your travels? How is it that we meet today, in this desert, among all this wailing? How did your travels go?" He opened his heart and told me all that had happened to him during our separation.

به قانون صحیح و بیان صریح محمدی و قرآنی ثابت و واضح است که در صورتی حج واجب و زیارت به موقع است که یک فقیر و ضعیف و گرسنه در همسایگی یا در بلد بلکه در تمام بلد بلکه در تمام ملت اسلام و ایران نباشد.

بیچاره! این دو برادر در خاک افتاده تضرع بسیار و التماس بیشمار نمودند که بارالها گناهان ما معلوم است و خطاهای ما مکشوف ولی ما در گروههای علمای غافل و کرورات فضلای جاهل دو تن بیش نیستیم، آنها نیز دخالت داشته اند و مراتب جهالت را می آراسته اند.

خطاب: مؤاخذات ما بر نوع شماست، ولی ایرادات نوعی بر افراد اشخاص نیز وارد است. کیفر همقطاران‌تان نیز داده شده و می شود، در دوزخ و دریای غضب ما بنگرید تا مشاهده نمائید کیفر رفتارها و مقام انتقامات ما را، گویا حجب برداشته و عوالم سدود انداخته شد، فضای بی منتهای دوزخ پیدا گشت. در شعله شدیده و زبان های عدیده و در سطح و قعر جهنم خوب نگریسته اغلب یا پیشوا می دیدم یا آقا یا واعظ مشاهده میکردم و معاینه حالت اغلب منقلب شد و اکثر مضطرب گردیدند. باز به حالت اولیه مراتب دوزخ غیرمرئی گردید.

خطاب رسید: دیدید و مشاهده کردید که بداندیش به سزای خود می رسد.

گفتند – خدایا – آنچه باید ببینیم دیدیم و آنچه باید به تقصیرات خود معترف هستیم.

در این بین یکی از دوستان صمیمی و یاران قدیمی را که چندی در مسافرت و سیاحت رفته بود دیدم. به طرف او دویدم دستش را گرفتم، گفتم جانم عزیزم در این مدت مسافرت چرا یادی از ما نکردی کاغذی ننوشتی، بریدی نفرستادی که حالا در این صحرای پرغوغا باید یکدیگر را ملاقات کنیم و از حال هم مستفسر شویم؟ بنای درد دل را گذاشت و شرح بیان سرگذشت مدت مفارقت خود را نمود.

We talked for a while, and were enjoying the conversation, when we heard a call being raised, announcing "Zell-al-Soltân, and the officials of Isfahan." I looked around, sorry that I had not paid attention to the accusations against the ulama. I asked a friend standing nearby, "What was the story with the two brothers? What did they do with the other notables of Isfahan?"

He said, "I was only paying attention while Sheykh Morteza Rizi was being accused, because during Ramadan of 1316 AH (1899) he declared that meat was forbidden. The sheep owners, who had lost their flocks to the cold weather during that month (January) as a result, were allied against him and demanded compensation for their losses."

"Why did the sheep die?" I asked.

He said, "They said, 'when we heard that the ulama had declared meat to be forbidden, we were outside the city. We turned back with our flocks to sell them in other cities, rather than take them to Isfahan and suffer loss. Three months on the road killed all our flocks.'"

"How much compensation did they seek?"

"I did not pay much attention, but there was talk of fifty or sixty thousand Tumans."

I said, "Briefly then, what happened?"

"Nothing. The Sheykh has been put with his colleagues."

"Hasn't the Friday prayer leader been summoned?"

He said, "I can't imagine why so many people attached themselves to him, when he was responsible for his servants' extortions, and his employees' injustice."

"So," I asked, "what happened in the end?"

He replied, "I did not follow it very well. However, I did understand that they blamed government officials for most of the errors, and that they sent a large number of the notables to the custodians of hell."

During these conversations, I kept my eyes on the foot of the scales of justice, waiting for the moment when Zell al-Soltân would favour the audience with his presence.

مدتی صحبت کردیم و سرگرم صحبت بودیم، یک وقت شنیدیم ندائی رسید:

ظل السلطان و کارگذاران اصفهان:
سر بالا کردم و افسوس خوردم که چرا ملتفت مواخذات از علما نشدم. از رفیق پهلوئی پرسیدم حال دو برادر چه شد، با سایر آقایان اصفهان چه کردند؟
گفت: من فقط در وقتی که از شیخ مرتضی ریزی در باب حرام کردن گوشت در رمضان سنه ۱۳۱۶ مواخذات می کردند و گله دارانی که به آن واسطه گوسفندهاشان در سرمای زمستان تلف شده بود به او آویخته بودند و غرامات ضررهای خود را می خواستند ملتفت بودم. گفتم چرا تلف شده بودند؟ گفت: گفتند ما چون در خارج شنیدیم که گوشت را علما حرام کرده اند گوسفندهای خود برگردانیدیم که بشهرهای دیگر راه به فروش برسانیم و وارد اصفهان ننمائیم که ضرر ببریم، سه ماه طول راه تمام گوسفندانمان را کشت.
گفتم چقدر مطالبه خسارت کردند؟ گفت درست ملتفت نشدم ولی گفتگوی پنجاه، شصت هزار تومان بود. گفتم: خوب مختصر بگو که چه شد؟ گفت هیچ آقا را نیز به همقطارانش ملحق کردند. گفتم: آقای امام جمعه احضار نشدند؟ گفت چرا عدۀ کثیری به ایشان آویخته بودند و بیشتر اجحافات نوکرها و ظلم مستخدمین او را دنبال داشتند. گفتم: بالاخره چه شد؟ گفت من چندان مستحضر نشدم. همین قدر فهمیدم که اغلب تقصیرها را راجع به کارگذاران حکومت کردند و عدۀ کثیری هم از آقایان را به مالک دوزخ سپردند.
در ضمن این مذاکره چشم به پای میزان حساب دوخته بودم که ظل سلطان تشریف فرما می شوند.

I saw a crowd in the distance, thronging together. There was a cloud of dust; it was chaos. When I looked closely, I saw that it was the pageantry of a procession. There was the prince, in his four-horse carriage, with a coachman sitting in front, and ten Persian Cossack horsemen with their leader Gholâm-Rezâ Khan Mohâjer riding behind the carriage. Ten or fifteen or more of his personal servants and staff followed the carriage, and in the distance we saw people with letters of complaint in their hands. The leader of the Cossacks took the letters and I wondered what answer would be given to these poor people. Finally, I saw the carriage before the scales of justice. The door opened. I saw Qâ'âni (Persian poet, 1807–53), standing near to the scales and reciting in a beautiful loud voice:

> Recite the Surah for Protection (Koran 114), the Devil has come from the well.
> Say, "there is no power and strength but in God"[70] for the little demon has come.

The Voice said, "O Mas'ud Mirzâ (governor of Isfahan), look at this limitless plain, and see this endless crowd. See how spacious it is, how crowded it is! They are all gathered here to be called to account for their deeds, for interrogation and punishment. Can your mind encompass such an event? Can you imagine what will happen on this day?"

His Highness rubbed his eyes and face, like a person who has just awoken. He yawned and looked around. When he saw that phenomenal sight, he became bewildered and shouted to his servant, "Jalil Âqâ Khan, water, bring water!"

The Voice said, "Here you are on the Plain of Resurrection, not in the gallery of your palace Bagh-e Now."

از دوردست محشر دیدم ازدحامی است و گرد و انقلابی، خوب نگریستم دیدم کوکبه جلال و موکب اجلال است. شاهزاده در کالسکهٔ چهاراسب، یکی از پیشخدمتها در جلو کالسکه نشسته ده سوار قزاق ایرانی با یاور آنها غلام رضاخان مهاجر عقب کالسکه می تازند. زیاده از ده و پانزده نفر دیگر پیشخدمت و مستخدمین شخصی دنبال کالسکه افتاده میآیند. از دور که نمایان بود، چند عریضه و شکایت نامه بعضی در دست داشتند، یاور قزاقها از آنها میگرفت، ملتفت نمی شدم که جواب آن بیچاره ها چه می شد. باری کالسکه رسید دم میزان حساب ایستاد. در کالسکه باز شد قاآنی را دیدم که در نزدیکی میزان ایستاده با صدائی بلند و آوازی دلپسند می گوید

تعویذ بگوئید که شد اهرمن از چاه
لاحول بخوانید که غولک بدر آمد

خطاب: ای مسعود میرزا نظر کن این صحرا و مخلوق نامتناهی را و ملاحظه نما این فضا و ازدحام نامعدود الهی را که تمام حاضرند برای دادن محاسبات اعمال خویش، و همگی آورده شده اند بجهت مواخذات و کیفر و مجازات خود، آیا امروز را بتصور راه میدادی و این هنگامه را بتخیل همراه میکردی؟

حضرت والا، دستی به چشم و صورت مالیده مثل کسیکه از خواب برخاسته خمیازه ای کشید نظر به اطراف محشر انداخته و در مشاهدهٔ آن خود را باخته فریاد کرد جلیل آقاخان پیشخدمت آب، آب.

خطاب: اینجا صحرای محشر است. کالاری باغ (گالری) باغ نو نیست.

He became more aware, but then anxiety and depression made him writhe, and he cried again, "Chamberlain!"

Someone close to him said, "Your Highness, you will meet him soon in a special place."

"Moshir-al-Molk!" he screamed. One of those with him said, "Do not call him, he will come looking for you."

"Sârem-al-Dowle, Banân-al-Molk, Mozaffar-al-Molk…" he shouted, calling all the officials of the Governor's office. Each time, someone explained where they were.

An angel appeared in human form and said to him, "Your Highness, this is not Isfahan, this is the Plain of Resurrection. What's wrong with you? This is the place of interrogation. You must answer yourself. Moshir-al-Molk and Banân-al-Molk cannot help you."

The Voice said, "Do not be so afraid, Mas'ud Mirzâ, do not give up. Today is not the day on which the help of others will be of any benefit to you, or in which fear will have any effect. Neither the Mullahs of Isfahan, nor consultations with anyone, will solve your problem. Today is the Day of Judgement, and the time of reckoning. Tell us what thanks you gave for our favours, and what good deeds you have done."

His Highness saw that there was but one thing to do, and no other way out but flattery. In despair, he uttered a prayer, "My Lord, this servant has been granted all kinds of favours; this humble one has received all kinds of bounties. You gave me prosperity and fortune, you made me a governor, and gave me intelligence." He threw himself on the ground, sobbing deeply. "O Lord, I did not serve you or your creatures. You know all my actions. Grant me compassion, because my deeds are ugly beyond imagination. Forgive me, do not punish me. All praise you for your compassion and compliment your kindness."

Suddenly I saw the poet Rumi (1207–73), who was saying with great truth and accuracy,

قدری بیشتر هوشیار شده اضطراب و پریشان حالی در پیچ و تابش انداخته صدا زد: صاحب دیوان!
شخصی بگوشش گفت حضرت والا، عنقریب در مقر مخصوصی ایشان را ملاقات می کنید. فریاد کرد: مشیرالملک! محرمی گفت که او را طلب مکن که او خود دنبال تو خواهد آمد. بانگ زد: صارم الدوله، بنان الملک و مظفرالملک و غیره و غیره و غیره... هی صدا زد و هر یک را کسی بعنوانی حالشان را بدو حالی کرد. ملکی به صورت انسان آمده گفت: حضرت والا اینجا اصفهان نیست. اینجا صحرای محشر است... شما را چه می شود! مقام بازخواست است. مشیرالملک و بنان الملک اینجا به کار نمی خورد. شخصاً باید جواب دهید.
خطاب رسید: مسعود میرزا مضطرب مشو انقلاب مدار که امروز روزی نیست که امداد غیر برایت ثمر کند و یا توحش و اضطراب اثری بخشد. نه ملاهای اصفهان به کارت می خورند و نه تدبیرات این و آن چاره به حالت می نمایند. امروز روز جزاست و زمان وانفسا، بگو بدانیم چه شکر نعمتی کردی و چه حسن خدمتی بجا آوردی؟ حضرت والا چاره را منحصر دیدن و راه مفر را مسدود فهمیدند، زبان به چاپلوسی بازکردند و بیان را بطور مأیوسی آغاز نمودند:
مناجات. الهی همه نوع نعمت شامل حال این بنده بود، همه قسم رحمت حاصل این شرمنده گشته، مکنتم دادی، دولتم عطا فرمودی، ریاست عنایت کردی، فراستم مرحمت نمودی، صورتم به خاک می مالید و زار می نالید که بارالها نه هیچ معرفتی در حقت حاصل کردم و نه هیچ منفعتی به خلقت رسانیدم، انچه کرده ام هم عنایت و ترحم نما که قبایح اعمالم بیش از آنست که تفکر گردد. بر من ببخشای و عذابم مفرمای که ترحمت را همه تحسین خوانند و تلطفت را جمله آفرین گویند.
ناگاه ملای رومی را دیدم که با جمال تحقیق و کمال تدقیق می گوید:

> You do bad deeds and greedily expect good in return.
> Surely the reward for a bad deed is bad.
> Despite God's generosity and compassion,
> You will not reap wheat, if you sow barley.

The Voice said, "We see into the innermost heart of every person, and we know what lies within the stone and clay. Here, a hypocritical plea will not be answered, there is no use in relying on dissimulation. One moment of sincere silence is better than a hundred years of lying humility. Tell us what you've done to our creatures, who were under your authority. What have you done due to combat oppression and evil?"

"O Lord, when you gave me absolute authority and entrusted several provinces to me, I was aware of, and upheld, the ranks necessary to social order, and the forms of retribution, for the sake of the peace of the ordinary people. My energy and efforts were beyond reproach, as everyone knows and many can testify."

The Voice said, "Do you imagine that we did not know your condition, your motivations and behaviour, or that we have closed our eyes to our servants? Is it not true that when we gave you power, your only goal was to satisfy your personal desires? Were you not careless regarding the very existence of a number of people? Was there a single beautiful woman under your protection, who did not fear for her chastity? What wealthy man had any rest from the burdens you imposed? How many houses did you amass? How many lineages did you annihilate?"

"O God," he replied, "you know me. I had little involvement in these matters. These people make a mountain out of a molehill."

Once again, the poet Sa'di stood erect, preparing himself, and said:

> If the king eats an apple from the garden of one of his subjects,
> his servants [following his example] will uproot the whole tree.

بد میکنی و نیک طمع میداری
خود بد باشد سزای بدکرداری
با آنکه خداوند کریم است و رحیم
گندم ندهد بار چو جو میکاری

خطاب رسید: مسعود میرزا از کنه هر دلی آگاهیم و بر درون هر سنگ و گلی گواه، اینجا تمنای تلبیس ثمری نبخشد و تولای تدلیس اثری ندهد. یک آن سکوت صادقانه به از صد سال خضوع کاذبانه است.
بازگو که با مخلوق من که در تحت اقتدار تو بودند چه کردی، از رفع ظلم و رفع شر چه هدیه آوردی؟
جواب: الهی وقتی که اقتدار کامله ام داده بودی و ایالات عدیده بدستم سپرده بودی مراتب انتظام و مراسم انتقام را در راحت رعیت و دفع اذیت حفظ می نمودم و در زحمت و کوشش رفع تهمت بودم چنانچه همه آگاهند و بسیاری گواه.
خطاب: آیا تو گمان می کنی ما از حالات و عوالمات و رفتارت بیخبر بوده ایم یا چشم از بندگان خود پوشیده ایم. مگر نه تو در هنگام اقتداری که بتو دادیم قصدت اجرای خیالات شخصی خود بود؟ مگر نه هستی گروهی را به باد دادی، کدام زن خوبرویی در ادرارت از عصمت خود وحشتناک نبود؟ کدام شخص با تمول از دهشت بردباری خود خواب آسوده داشت؟ چه خانه ها را که برچیدی چه طایفه ها را که نابود کردی.
جواب: بار پروردگارا من خود تو میدانی کمتر در آن اقدامات بوده ام، اگر یکی بوده ده گفته اند و اگر حرفی بوده کلامی ننموده اند.
اینجا نیز سعدی شیرازی قد راست کرده خود را آراسته نموده فریاد کرد:

اگر ز باغ رعیت ملک خورد سیبی
برآورند غلامان او درخت از بیخ

The Voice said, "If you had no intentions against the chastity of my servants, why did you attend the wakes and other meetings for women? If you were not coveting the property and wealth of the people, to confiscate them, how did you amass all this land, all these houses and all this money?" While these accusations were being made, I saw that a number of people came out of the crowd. There was a murmuring and grumbling. One of these people said, "Before, he had the power, and we said nothing, for fear of our lives. Now we will at last get it back, and double."

Another said, "At that time, he confiscated wealth by force; now we may see whether my documents or his have more weight."

Another said, "I have a document from Sheykh Mohammad Bâqer."

Another said, "I have a warrant from the Seyyed."

Another, "I have the testimony of the common people."

Another, "I have the fatwas of the ulama."

Another, "My father."

Another, "My brother."

One had a general claim, one had proof of his losses. One spoke of a thousand tumans, another of a hundred thousand, and yet another of five hundred thousand. In the end, a large crowd had gathered at the foot of the scales of justice, each of them with a claim.

The Gracious Voice said, "Answer each of these questions, for your excuses are not accepted and delay is not permitted." His Highness was gripped by a strange confusion, and then a remarkable transformation came over him. He ignored all that had happened previously, and the reproofs delivered against the distinguished ulama of Isfahan (may God have mercy on them).

At this point, his eye fell on the group of plaintiffs, and he saw Mirzâ ʿAbd-al-Wahhâb, who was first in line. He called him and said: "Speak to the distinguished ulama of Isfahan on my behalf, and say, 'It comes to this, O… : I helped you in many ways, in Isfahan, I made you wealthy, and powerful, owners of villages and towns, and storehouses.

خطاب: اگر تو بعصمت بندگان من صمع نداشتی در تعزیه و جمعیت زنانه چه اقدامی داشتی؟ اگر تو مال و ملک مردم را در صدد اخذ و ظبط نبودی، با کدام مواجب و خدمت این املاک و عمارات و این وجوهات و نقود را حاصل کردی؟
در میان این مواخذات دیدم متصل بعضی از جمعیت خارج می شوند، غرغرکنان و لندلند زنان یکی می گوید آنوقت اقتدار داشت از ترس جانمان حرف نمیزدیم، حالا با اجرت المثل پس می گیریم. یکی می گفت آن زمان مجبوراً ضبط کرد، حالا ببینیم اسناد من معتبرتر است یا سند مالکیت او، یکی می گفت نوشته از شیخ محمد باقر دارم، یکی می گفت سند از سید دارم، یکی می گفت استشهاد عام دارم، یکی می گفت استفتا از علما دارم، یکی می گفت پدرم دیگری می گفت برادرم، یکی ادعای تمامی داشت یکی سند بربادی در میآورد، یکی از هزار حرف میزد، یکی از صدهزار می گفت، یکی از کرور صحبت می داشت بالاخره جمعیتی زیاد در پای میزان حساب حاضر شده هر یک ادعائی میکردند.
خطاب مستطاب رسید: جواب یک یک اینها را بازگوی که عذر مسموع نیست و تعلل مرفوع است.
اضطراب عجیبی حضرت والا را دست داد و انقلاب غریبی بر ایشان عارض گشت. از مقدمات سابقه و سرگذشت مؤاخذات علمای اعلام اصفهان وفق الله آرائهم مستحضر نبودند و در این ضمن چشمشان به جرگه دبنگوزها افتاد میرزا عبدالوهاب را دید که در سر آن سلسله است احضارش فرموده گفت برو نزد اقایان علمای اصفهان از قول من بگو ای ... در اصفهان همه نوع همراهی با شما نمودم، صاحب پولتان کردم، صاحب دولت و ده و قریه و قصبه و انبارتان نمودم،

'Remember the promises you gave me secretly, the plans we stitched together in private? It was all done with foresight of a day such as this, these strategies were all planned for an hour like the present. Now at last, help me! Do something!' Explain my predicament to them in detail. May God bless you, may my life be a sacrifice for you, truly. I hope you can make them act in such a way that they stop this game within half an hour. My friend, I have signed and stamped documents. They are with Mirzâ Bâqer Khan, the secretary."

The assayer said, "It is now obvious that the mind of His Highness is not focused on the realm of the gathering of souls, and the resurrection in ranks. He says, 'they will stop this game!'"

The Voice said, "What is your answer, what excuse do you have?"

"Judgement belongs to the King," he answered. "I am not involved at all, I do not interfere in these matters. His Excellency Rokn-al-Molk and the Mollâbâshi are in the Ministry of Justice. Write a petition to them, and they will note their response in their own hand in the margin, concerning [your] rights." It appeared that the message he had sent to the notables had given him a degree of self-confidence.

The Voice said, "Mas'ud Mirzâ, this is not Isfahan! When will you understand? This is the Court of the Last Judgement. It's about you, not about the petitions and grievances of the people of Isfahan. Here, there is retribution, not complaining about various matters. This is the Plain of the Gathering of Souls, not the portico, palace or sheltering grove."

Meanwhile, His Highness saw Mirzâ ʿAbd al-Wahhâb. Silently, with eyes and hands, he asked what the response from the notables had been, what steps they had taken, what Mirzâ ʿAbd al-Wahhâb had done. The latter gave him a sign with hand and chin, meaning, 'Nothing!' His Highness made the sign with his fingers that means, 'How so?' He said: 'It is going wrong.' He asked: 'Didn't you see them?' Mirzâ said: 'Yes I did.' He asked: 'Where?' Mirzâ said: 'If you wait, I will see to it.' He said: 'Come a few steps closer, so that I can hear what you are saying.'

چه قولها که محرمانه به من داده اید چه دوزها که مخفیانه با هم چیده ایم تمام برای همچو روزی این پیش بینی بوده بجهت چنین ساعتی این خیال اندیشی شده، آخرای بی همتمان دستی بجنبانید، کاری بکنید، تفصیل گرفتاری مرا برایشان نقل کن. بارک الله قربانتم ها، دلم می خواهد به قسمی که می دانی چنان مردشان کنی که نیمساعت طول نکشد که تمام این بازیها را بهم بزنند جانمی رقم خالصه گی ملک را مهر و امضا کردم پیش میرزا باقرخان منشی باشی است.

تحقیق: معلوم می شود هنوز خاطر مبارک حضرت مستطاب والا بعوالم حشر و مراتب نشر مقر و مطمئن نشده می فرماید این بازیها را به هم بزنند.

خطاب آمد که: جوابت چیست، عذرت کدامست؟

جواب: بملک خطاب آورنده دادند. منکه حالتی ندارم و دخالتی در امورات نمی کنم. جناب رکن الملک و ملاباشی در محاکمه دیوانخانه هستند. مطالب را بنویسید تا حاشیه اش دستخط شود رسیدگی و احقاق نمایند. گویا پیغامیکه به آقایان داده اند قدری ایشان را مطمئن نموده.

خطاب: مسعود میرزا اینجا اصفهان نیست. تا کی حالی نمی شوی، اینجا مقام بازخواست است، این خطاب با تست عرایض و تظلمات اهل اصفهان نیست، این مواخذات است تشکی امورات نیست، اینجا صحرای محشر است، گالری عمارت و باغ کاج نیست.

چشم حضرت والا در بین این استماعات به میرزا عبدالوهاب افتاد با دست و چشم اشاره کردند جواب و اقدام آقایان چه شد؟ چه کردی؟ با دست و چانه اشاره کرد هیچ. به انگشتان فهماندند چطور؟ وچند قدمی نزدیک شد و گفت کار خراب است. گفتند مگر ندیدی آنها را؟ گفت چرا تماشان را. گفتند کجا؟ گفتند تامل بفرمایید خدمتشان خواهیم رسید. گفتند نزدیک بیا بشنوم چه میگوئی.

When they were closer, Mirzâ ʿAbd al-Wahhâb said, "Give up hope."

His Highness asked, "What do you mean?"

He replied, "I've seen those gentlemen, they were drowned in the sea of divine wrath."

His Highness said, "But what is going on?"

He replied, "Hola! Have you still not understood? This is the time and place of the Resurrection! Those gentlemen have already been summoned to appear, and they have all received their sentences. The odd thing is that some of them put the blame on your Highness."

His Highness said, "What are you talking about!"

He replied, "Just what I said. If there's more to it, you would know."

The Voice said, "Mas'ud Mirzâ, this is not Iran. Your connections in worldly affairs are no more. There's no point in setting one or other plan into motion. Even if you write a hundred letters to Tehran, dispatch a thousand agents in the cities of Iran or send hundreds of thousands[71] to notables in the various regions, we cannot conceal faults or choose not to punish them. O Mas'ud, do you want me to reveal all your secrets and requite all your deeds?"

Since His Highness could not find a single one of his servants and assistants, and had obtained no help from the notables or from his officials, he gave a sigh, expressing helplessness, dejection and submission to necessity, and replied, "I do not want that, and I never foresaw the utter disgrace I am in."

The Voice said, "But when you became governor of Isfahan, you put no limits on your own powers: in fact, did you limit yourself in anything?"

"I admit it," he said.

نزدیک شده گفت مأیوس باشید.
گفتند برای چه؟
گفت حضرات را دیدم که در دریای آتش غضب الهی غوطه ور بودند. گفتند مگر چه حکایتی است؟
گفت به به هنوز نفهمیده اید که مقام و روز قیام قیامت است. حضرات احضار شدند و بکیفر خود گرفتار گردیدند و تعجب در آن که بعضی تقصرات را نیز راجع بحضرت والا نموده اند.
گفتند چه می گوئی، گفت چنین است که می گویم دیگر خود دانید.
خطاب رسید: مسعود میرزا اینجا ایران نیست و تعلقات امور دنیوی منتفی است. تحریکات این و آن بکار نمی خورد. صد کاغذ اگر به طهران بنویسی یا هزار محرک اگر به شهر های ایران روانه نمائی یا کرور ها به آقایان بلدان تقدیم کنی تقصیرات ما را نمی توانی جلوگیری نمائی و تنبیهات ما را نمی شود بیهوده گذاری.
یا مسعود می خواهی تا اسرارت را تمام اظهار دارم و افعالت را همه انتقام کشم؟
از نوکران و پیشکاران خود کسی را نیافته از آقایان و تدبیرات خویش ثمری نبرده، مأیوسانه با عجز و انکسار و لابه و اضطرار عرض کرد: هیچ چنین خواهشی را نخواهم و ابداً این افتضاح را چشمداشت ندارم.
خطاب رسید: مگر وقتی که به حکومت اصفهان آمدی دارائی خود را تهدید نکردی، مگر جز دارای هیچ بودی؟
جواب: چنین است.

The Voice said, "Did we not make you the son of the King (Nâser-al-Din Shah)?"
"You did."

The Voice said, "Did we give you servants and officials such as Sâheb Divân, Sârem-al-Dowle, Banân-al-Molk, Mozaffar al-Molk, Moshir-al-Molk and the like…?"

"Yes."

"Did you not have a shrewd and skilful official, in Ebrâhim Khalil Khan, and others like him?"

"He was also a Turk."

"Were you not the leading landowner?"

"What are you accusing me of?"

"Were you not rich?"

"Unless the English banks delay or block payments, as happened to Seyyed Baqr, who had his liquid assets in those parts."

"Did you not have children, and a large family?"

"Cursed be their father, these children and family will ruin me."

"Did you not have a son, the like of Jalâl-al-Dowle?"

"But he proved to be worthless."

"Despite certain matters, which you know of, and certain activities, which we know about, did we not reappoint you to a position of leadership and responsibility, after the death of your father?"

"I wore my tongue out in flattery and servility."

"Were you not honored by the King at the beginning of each year, with a robe and fine words?"

"My heart burns to think how much money I gave out in gratuities!"

"If you can find excuses for these matters, with respect to the [provincial] government in which you had absolute power, why did you not recognize the rights of the poor? You never gave people their real entitlements. What did you do about the

خطاب: تو را پسر سلطان ایران نکردیم؟
جواب: چرا.
خطاب: پیشکاران و نوکرهائی مثل صاحب دیوان و صارم الدوله و بنان الملک و مظفر الملک و مشیر الملک و غیره و غیره به تو ندادیم؟
جواب: چنین است.
خطاب: نوکری مثل ابراهیم خان زرنگ و کارکن نداشتی؟
جواب: ترک هم بود.
خطاب: اول ملاک نشدی؟
جواب: اگر مواخذات تو بگذارد
خطاب: دولتمند نشدی؟
جواب: اگر بانکهای انگلیس مثل وجوه نقد سید باقر که در آن نقاط داشت در ادایش اهمال و حاشا نکنند.
خطاب: صاحب طایفه و اولاد نشدی؟
جواب: بر پدرشان لعنت که هم این اولاد و طایفه مرا خانه خراب خواهند کرد.
خطاب: پسری مثل جلال الدوله نداری؟
جواب: اگر نااهل نباشد.
خطاب: با وجود آن مراتب که می دانی و اقداماتی که می دانیم پس از فوت پدرت باز بریاست و حکومت نایل نبودی؟
جواب: تملق و چاپلوسی زبانم را سائیده.
خطاب: هر سال اول موقع به خلعت و مرحمتی از طرف شاه نائل نشدی؟
جواب: بسکه پول به اجزا دادم جگرم خون شد.
خطاب: اگر این مراتب را عذر می آوری در حوزۀ حکومت خود که اقتدار تامه داشته ای پس چرا حق فقرا را منظور نمی آورده، ابداً احقاق حقی نمی کرده

increase in poverty and scarcity, the proliferation of foolishness and ignorance, the pervasive oppression and confusion among my servants, who were under your leadership?"

"O God," he replied, "Because I knew nothing of these occurrences and I did not believe in the Resurrection of the Dead or the Last Judgement, or the interrogation and accusation. On earth, whatever I did, whatever... no one said a word or raised a question or called me to account. My God, that was the sort of religious leaders we had, as you can see!"

Rumi intervened again, to put the complaints in precise words. He recited this verse,

> When the pathfinder is off the path so widely
> How can his disciple find the path to paradise?

The Voice said, "Mas'ud Mirzâ, such excuses are not acceptable here. This is no way to answer the oppressed and the poor. This is the Court of Justice, it is not affected by excuses and obfuscations. You benefited from so much compassion and blessings in your life, but you have shown just as much ingratitude in turning away from them. How long would you have kept oppressing them, how long would you have continued to punish them?"

Just when Mas'ud Mirzâ was ready to answer, the whole audience, each of whom had a sealed document and a complaint, each with a plea and a desire for redress, began jostling one another frenetically. An enormous uproar arose. For fear of being crushed, I took refuge in a corner. I saw Jahângir Khan the Turk, who had spent his time in Isfahan, studying science, philosophy and religious principles, who had attained learning and yet wore his old clothing and hat. I asked him, "What are you doing here, Sir?"

He replied, "They wanted to draw me into the crowd of notables you can see. I've taken refuge here. May God have mercy on me!"

As we talked, I came to understand what he meant.

Translation of The True Dream 93

ازدیاد فقر و گرانی و انبساط حمق و نادانی و انتشار ظلم و پریشانی در بندگان من که مرئوست بوده اند به چه علت داده ای؟
جواب: بار پروردگارا منکه این مقامات را نمی دانستم و معتقد نبودم که عوالم حشری و مواخذه ای، یا مراتب نشری و مطالبة باشد. در دنیا هم که هر چه می کردم یا هر .... می نمودم کسی نبود که حرفی زند یا جهتی پرسد یا مواخذه نماید. خدایا آن پیشوایان مذهبی ما بودند که دیدی.
ملای رومی باز از آستین دستی در آورده در پوستین تحقیق بسطی داد و زبان گشاد که آری:

هر کرا پیش چنین گمره بود
کی مریدش را به جنت ره بود

خطاب رسید: مسعودمیرزا این عذرها در این مقام پذیرفته نیست، جواب مظلومین و فقرا را به این اقسام نمی توان داد. اینجا مقام محاکمة عدالت است نه مورد اعتذار و کنایت. مراتب ترحم و تفضل تا به چه اندازه با تو همراهی کرده و تو در کفران آن با به چه درجه اغماض کرده ای، ظلم تا کی تعدی تا چند.
تا جواب را خواستند ادا نمایند جمعیت منتظر که هر کس سند و حرفی داشت و هرکدام ادعا و حقی مطالبه می نمودند ازدحام بی اندازه کرده غوغائی فوق العاده برخاست. از ترس اینکه مبادا پامال شوم به کناری دویدم. جهانگیرخان ترک را که در اصفهان به تحصیل علم و حکمت و اصول کوشش نموده با علم و کمال هنوز در لباس اصلی خود و کلاه باقی است دیدم. پرسیدم آقا شما اینجا چه می کنید؟
گفت مرا هم می خواستند داخل جرگة آقایان که مشاهده کردی نمایند فرار کرده و اینجا پناه آورده، مگر خدا ترحم فرماید. قدری مشغول صحبت شدیم وقتی ملتفت شدم که

The Voice said, "Summon Rokn-al-Molk and the Mollâbâshi, Mirzâ Hasan-'Ali Khan, Mirzâ Bâqer Khan and Mirzâ Asadollâh Khan." I found no trace of His Highness among that crowd of the rich and famous, although I searched and made enquiries. When I asked, they answered that he had been obliterated at a stroke, under the weight of his cunning schemes and the long list of his deceits. Not a trace remained of him. I did not know where he had gone, or rather, where he was hiding.

In my dream, I went searching for him. I wanted to understand what had happened in his case and what the outcome was. I went around in the crowd, attentively looking at each group. I saw a group of gentlemen traders, and a bunch of great dignitaries. In each group, there were people of the same station and occupation. In one group, between the others, I came upon a group of ruffians. I saw their leader Hâjji Seyyed 'Abd al-Wahhâb Shams-Âbâdi. In the group of rogues, I saw Âqâ Mirzâ Mohammad-'Ali from the Hakimi mosque. I came to one group that I did not recognize. I asked about them, and someone told me, "They do everything: corruption, murder, pillage and maliciousness. They do all sorts of things like this, all the time! They lend money with interest!"

Much surprised, I looked around and saw one group whose name is avoided with a euphemism. Among them I saw Molla 'Ali-Akbar Fashâraki. As soon as he saw me, he left his fellows and followed me. He asked me for the remaining portion of an interest payment. Quite alarmed, I sought refuge among the crowd. Gradually, I worked my way towards the scales of justice to see the disputes and the reckoning. I arrived just as the censure was pronounced.

The Voice said, "Soleymân Khan Rokn-al-Molk, were you not the vicegerent of the government? You were responsible for good order in the city, were you not?"

"My God," he replied, "as I indicated, all the thieves and miscreants claimed to be allied to a notable or a mullah. No sooner did I begin to say something or to inflict retribution than I received thousands of letters from the notables, who said that this person

خطاب رسید: حاضر کنید رکن الملک و ملاباشی و میرزا حسنعلیخان و میرزا باقر خان و میرزا اسدالله خان را.

هر چه تفحص کردم و تجسس نمودم از کوکبهٔ جلال و کبکبهٔ اجلال حضرت والا نشانه ای نیافتم. پرسیدم، گفتند در تحت تدبیرات و ذیل تدلیسات خود یک مرتبه محو و معدوم شده. اثری از ایشان باقی و نشانه ای از وجودشان مرئی نشده نفهمیدم به کجا رفتند و در کدام نقطه مخفی گردیدند.

خیالات خواب در صدد تفتیش و جستجوی ایشانم انداخت که رفته حال و نتیجه را مستحضر کردم. در این جمعیت و گروه گردش میکردم و چهار چشم هر فرقه را نظاره مینمودم. گروهی حضرات تجار را دیدم. دسته ای اقایان عظام را مشاهده کردم. هر جمعیتی را می دیدم که با همقطاران خود دسته شدند. بدستهٔ فیمابین الواط رسیدم حاجی سید عبدالوهاب شمس آبادی را دیدم سرکرده است. به گروه مشدیان و داشان آقا میرزا محمدعلی مسجد حکیمی را دیدم در آن جرگه است. به گروهی رسیدم و نشناختم، پرسیدم گفتند اینها همه کاره‌اند. فساد، قتل، غارت، شرارت، همه نوع از این قبیل کارها را دارند. ضمناً پول هم نفع می دهند.

با کمال تعجب نگریستم جمعی را دیدم که اسم بردن آنها ریا می شود. از آن میان ملا علی اکبر فشارکی را دیدم به محض اینکه چشمش به من افتاد همقطاران خود را نهاده و مرا دنبال نموده مطالبهٔ جزئی بقیهٔ فرع را میکند. من مضطرب شده در میانه جمعیت پنهان شدم. کمک کم خود را نزدیک میزان حساب کشیدم که مبارزات و مواخذات را تماشا کنم. در وسط مواخذات بود رسیدم.

خطاب رسید: سلیمان خان رکن المک، مگر نایب الحکومه نبودی و انتظام شهر بدستت نبود؟

جواب: بار پروردگارا عرض کردم که هر یک از سارقین یا تعدی کنندگان خود را به آقائی بسته یا به ملائی آویخته بودند نه به حرف میخواستم بزنم یا کیفر که میخواستم بدهم از آقایان هزار کاغذ می رسید که

should appear only before the shariah court. Even if the theft and the identity of the thief were public knowledge, in the end the thief would swear an oath, and that was the end of the matter."

The Voice said, "Give us the other reason; hide nothing from us."

"I swear on my father's soul that I have never sought the property of others. Yet you say that I shut my eyes when I knew of a theft! I must tell you, one day, when these worthless princes (he turns towards hell) were senior officials, I gave the order to keep the shops open and no one had the courage to contradict me. Yes, I am that man."

The Voice said, "If someone else did something, what does that have to do with you? We asked you about thefts by thieves and the pleas for justice from the oppressed. We do not want stories and tales. Explain where the stolen property is and how you have punished the thieves."

"I tell you, I have been in office for forty years now. I swear on the soul of my father (Khalaf Beyk) that I suffered severe wrongs and injuries. Anyone whose property had been stolen or whose house was broken into would come to me with his complaints. There were an incredible number of complaints. Oh, oh, oh so many things happened! Zell-al-Soltân did not give me the instructions, but these people in Isfahan did what they did. 'Protect your assets, lest they be stolen by a thief who is not hidden in my sleeve.' How well it is said, 'the rough and the soft get along very well.'"[72] He turned to someone I did not know, and recited this line.

The Voice said, "Soleymân Khan of Shiraz, you wanted to compose poetry. Are you trying to tell us that you were like the other poets, taking pride in an empty stomach and living in poverty in Shiraz with one wooden spoon, a water pipe and

فلانی در محضر شرع باید حاضر شود. با وجودیکه سرقت و سارق هم مفهوم عامه بوده بالاخره سارق را قسم می دادند و مسئله ختم می شد.
خطاب: علل دیگرش را هم ذکر کن. چیزی را از ما پنهان مدار.
جواب: به ارواح پدرم نه په من هیچ طمع به مال کسی نکرده بودم نه په خیال می کنید من از دزدی کسی با خبر باشم و چشم بپوشم؟ من بشما بگویم یکوقت همین حضرت والا نه په ها (رو کرد به طرف دوزخ) ادارات باش بود حکم می شد همه دکانها را باز بگذارند. مگر کسی جرئت داشت، بله من همین آدمم.
خطاب: کسی دیگر کاری میکرده چه ربطی بعالم تو داشته. ما از سرقت سارقین و دادخواهی مظلومین می پرسیم قصه و حکایت نمی خواهیم بیان کنی، بگو اموال مسروقه کجاست و سارقین را در چه مجازات آوردی؟
جواب: من به شما بگویم حالا چهل سال است خدمت می کنم به ارواح پدرم (خلف بیگ) چقدر اذیت و صدمه می کشم هر کس مالش را می برند یا خانه اش را می چاپند، تعرضش را به من دارند (با حالت فوق العادهٔ تعرض) ای وی وی نپه خیلی حکایت است. ظل السلطان این تحکمات را به من نمی کند که این اصفهانیها می کنند. مالت را محافظت کن نبرند. دزد که توی آستین من نیست. چقدر خوب گفته است: درشتی و نرمی بهم بر خوش است.
رو کرده به کسیکه نشناختم این مصراع را خواند.
خطاب آمد: سلیمان خان شیرازی، شعر می خواستی بگوئی می خواستی مثل سایر شعرا پیه گرسنگی و ... خوردن را به خود بمالی در شیراز با یک چنته و غلیان و

a bit of hide to sit on? In fact, you had whatever you wanted. Give an answer, say how you protected the life and property, the honour and reputation of the people, when you were vicegerent in Isfahan."

His Excellency Rokn-al-Molk was struck by these aspersions on his character. His manner changed, and he reverted to the Shiraz dialect. He shouted, "Hoy, you fellows! Is there anyone there?"

He called Deputy 'Abd-al-Rahim, Deputy Rezâ, Deputy Ebrâhim, and some other deputies and officers by name. Finally, he saw Mirzâ Toghrol Khan and said, "Are none of these bastards here?"

"No, Sire."

He said, "Tell one of the boys to prepare my coach quickly. I will never be a servant! Cursed be on my father if I stay for one more hour. What can be achieved by all this?" He began to protest and complain.

The Voice said, "Soleymân Khan, this is not the seat of government in Isfahan, where if there was one unwelcome question regarding the affairs of Zell-al-Soltân, you could complain and call for your coach to be prepared, close your pen case, fasten your cloak and go home! This is where vengeance is exacted. You will be heard and punished, based on the extent to which you have eased the lives of your subjects and subordinates, on your judgements with respect to the needy, the weak and the helpless, and on whether you have restored stolen property to owners who cannot speak for themselves."

"What? Are you going to raise that again? Was I the people's guardian, or the accomplice of thieves in their theft?"

The Voice said, "You know very well, and so do we, as we have testified. Don't pretend to know nothing, or we will speak plainly."

Then his Excellency Rokn-al-Molk became very upset. He began to insult His Highness and said, "Cursed be my father if I

پوست تخت هر چه دلت میخواست بگوئی و بخوری. جواب ایام نایب الحکومه‌گی را بگوی که جان و مال و آبرو و ناموس مردم را چگونه محافظت کردی.
جناب رکن الملک با حالت شیرازی گری این حسابات به طبعشان گران آمده متغیر شدند و صدا کردند آهای بچه ها کیس اینجا نایب عبدالرحیم نایب رضا نایب ابراهیم چندین نایب و دهباشی اسم بردند عاقبت چشمشان بمیرزا طغرل خان افتاد گفتند این زن قحبه ها هیچیک اینجا نیستند؟ گفت خیر آقا. گفتند یکی از بچه ها را بگو زود کالسکه حاضر کند من دیگر ابداً نوکری نمی کنم، بر پدرم لعنت اگر ساعتی دیگر توقف نمایم، پیه این چه وضعی است. بنای تعرض و قال و مقال را گذاشتند.
خطاب رسید: سلیمان خان، اینجا دارالحکومه اصفهان نیست که محض مغلطه در بعضی اظهارات ظل السلطان تعرض کنی بگوئی کالسکه ات را حاضر نمایند و عبایت را با قلمدان بهم پیچیده بروی خانه ات. اینجا مورد انتقام است و از تو سئوال و مؤاخذه می شود که رفاهیت حال مرئوسین و محکومین خود را چگونه فراهم آوردی، دربارۀ فقرا و ضعفا و بیچارگان چطور حکم کردی، اموال غارت شده بینوایان را چگونه مسترد ساختی؟
جواب: پیه باز تکرار می شود. مگر من وکیل مردم بود. مگر من شریک دزدی و دزدها بودم.
خطاب: تو خود میدانی ما هم گواهیم آنقدر تجاهل مکن تا صریحاً بگوئیم.
بلی جناب رکن الملک متغیر شدند بنا کردند بحضرت والا بد گفتن .... بر پدرم لعنت اگر من

continue to serve Zell-al-Soltân. After forty years of service he has left me subject to these accusations."

He called Mirzâ Fath-'Ali Khan and told him, "Go to Zell-al-Soltân and tell him that I can no longer perform any of the tasks he instructed me to perform. In fact he should come now to answer questions. I have served him all this time, I have had several copies of the Koran printed, I raised him, and now I have to listen to stuff like this from these people."

The Voice said, "Soleymân Khan, even if you printed the Koran, what good is that, when your behaviour was in breach of its provisions? What was the benefit from all that ink and paper? If you had taken steps to promulgate its laws, some pride would be fitting. You have thrown the property of the people, the petitions of the helpless, the rights of the oppressed, the homes of the voiceless, the prosperity of my servants to the winds, putting everything at risk. Yet you are proud of forming an Islamic Association, saying your obligatory prayers in the mosque on time and publishing a few copies of the Koran?"

"Now, now, the establishment of the Islamic Association was no minor matter."

The Voice said, "Certainly it is no small thing, to destroy and endanger the wealth of the people and the public finances; to double your own holdings in the country; to make yourself infamous in Iran and elsewhere; to fill Hajji Mohammad Hossein Kazeruni with pride; to sow so much opium, which is a pillar of the [country's] trade and economy, that the market was weakened; and to sell the tobacco and opium of your helpless partners at half their value! If the company made any profit, it all went to your own account, and if there was any loss it was charged to the general account. Yes, all this is no small matter; it is a great betrayal and a serious matter."

"Oh! I swear on my father's soul that the ulama and the people appreciated my work, they reported it in the newspapers. The rich and powerful sent me letters of approval and congratulations. The people were full of praise and satisfied, and

دیگر نوکری ظل‌السلطان را بکنم بعد از چهل سال خدمت حالا مرا گیر مواخذات انداخته.

صدا زدند میرزا فتعلی خان را که برو پیش ظل السلطان. بگو من دیگر از عهده برنمیایم بکارهائی که مرا واداشتی، پیه حالا هم بیا جوابش را بده من از این مدت نوکری تو را کردم چند نسخه قران چاپ کردم من تو را بزرگت کردم حالا از این مردم باید این حرفها را گوش بدهم.

خطاب رسید: سلیمان خان نه قران خوب بود چاپ نمائی و نه بر ضد احکام آن رفتار کنی، در انتشار مرکب و کاغذ چه فایده است اقدام به رواج احکامش اگر کرده ای افتخار بایستی نمائی. مال مردم، عرض بیچارگان، حق مظلومان، خانه بینوایان، ثروت بندگان را بر باد داده، در خطر انداختهٔ و غره هستی که شرکت اسلامیه بر پا کرده ای یا نمازت را به وقت در مسجد خوانده ای یا چند جلد قران چاپ کرده ای.

جواب: په په شرکت اسلامیه کوچک کاری بود.

خطاب: البته ثروت مردم را پول عموم را در سوخت و خطر انداختن پارچه های مملکت خود را دوبرابر گران کردن خود را در انظار داخله و خارجه مفتضح نمودن، حاجی محمد حسین کازرونی را باد زیر بغل انداختن، تریاک که عمدهٔ تجارت و دخل داخله است گنجیدهٔ زیادی داخل کردن و رشتهٔ تجارت را به هم زدن، تنباکو و تریاک شرکای بیچاره را نیمه بها فروختن، اگر دخلی در کمپانی باشد بجمع تجارت شخصی خود درآوردن، اگر ضرری پیدا شود پای عموم ملت حساب کردن کوچک کاری نیست بلکه بزرگ خیانت و عظیم اقدامی است.

جواب: ای وای به ارواح پدرم علما و مردم تحسین این کار مرا کردند در روزنامه جات نوشتند و اعیان و ارکان کاغذ تحسین و آفرین فرستادند. ملت همه دعاگو و راضی بودند

now I am criticized!

The Voice said, "True enough. If only there had been newspapers in Iran that denounced your moral vices and mean behaviour. If only the people were not such stupid donkeys. If only the rich and powerful had put aside their personal ambitions. Then had there been consequences for these actions, all this would not have happened. Why is no one willing to buy the shares in the Islamic Association for even a third of their value?"

They were in the midst of this discussion when Mirzâ Toghrol Khan approached Rokn-al-Molk. He gave him some reassurance, saying: "Sir, don't take it too hard. Sir, don't be upset. This is not in question, really. How beautifully it has been said – listen carefully to hear the heights of poetic eloquence – last night I composed a poem on the same metre as the following:

> It's not beneficial for a secret to come from behind the veil,
> In the gathering of the mystics, there's nothing to see.

But, you see, all these complications have made me forget it. Anyway, can you tell me who wrote it?"

Toghrol Khan replied, "Isn't it by Hâtef of Isfahan, who says:

> Although our hidden dishonour's revealed
> and woe! We are shamed, and thrown in confusion,
> We're proud to be pious and rejoice in Islam:
> The Magi take issue because we are Muslims.

His Excellency Rokn-al-Molk nodded, and was preparing to recite a poem, when one of the servants of hell took on the form of Mirzâ Fath-'Ali Khan and said to him, "I have delivered your message word for word to His Highness, and he replied, 'Arouse yourself, and come here in person.'"

His Excellency Rokn-al-Molk said, "I will never again go to Zell-al-Soltân, I do not serve him."

نه به اینم حرف توش در آوردن.
خطاب: بلی اگر روزنامه جاتی در داخله بود که معایب اخلاق و رذایل رفتار شما را بیان می کرد یا اگر ملت احمق و خر نبود یا اگر اعیان و ارکان غرض شخصی را کنار گذاشته کیفر اعمال در کار بود این واقعات نبود، بلیط های شرکت اسلامیه را چرا حالا کسی ثلث بها نمی خرد و نمی دهد.
در این گفتگو بودند که میرزا طغرل خان نزدیک به جناب رکن الملک شده قدری تسلیت داده گفت آقا متحمل نشوید، آقا متغیر نباشید، اینها مسئله نیست واقعاً چقدر خوب گفته ملتفت باشید. ملاحت شعر تا چه اندازه است جناب رکن الملک نپه. منهم پریشب یک غزلی بر وزن غزل

مصلحت نیست که از پرده برون افتد راز
ورنه در مجلس رندان خبری نیست که نیست

گفته بودم. می بینی این گرفتاریها از یادم برده. خوب نپه بگو مال کیست؟
طغرل خان: مال هاتف اصفهانی ست. می گوید:

گر فاش شود عیوب پنهانی ما
ای وای بخجلت و پریشانی ما
ما غره بدین داری و شاد از اسلام
گبران متنفر از مسلمانی ما

جناب رکن الملک قدری سر تکان داده عازم خواندن غزل و شعری بودند که یکی از عمله جات دوزخ به شکل میرزا فتحعلی خان آمده و به جناب رکن الملک عرض کرد پیغامات را عیناً به حضرت والا عرض کردم، فرمودند خودتان تشریف بیاورید اینجا. جناب رکن الملک گفتند من دیگر پیش ظل السلطان نخواهم رفت، نوکری نمی کنم،

Outwardly, he adamantly refused, but since he wished it in his heart, Mirzâ Fath-'Ali Khan led him away to His Highness.

Then they led His Eminence the Mollâbâshi, Mirzâ Ahmad, the Chief astrologer, before the scales of justice. The Voice said, "Do you remember the time when you had no income or assets, and you brought your handwritten almanac to Tehran, seeking through it to gain an appointment from the pillars of the state?"

He smiled, bowing low, and muttered between clenched teeth, "What's your point?"

The Voice said, "Despite your stupidity and your strange appearance, have we not given you wealth? Have we not made you an important member of the government? Did we not grant you power? Did we not grant you all the dues of the treasury of Isfahan? Did we not put Zell-al-Soltân's rental income, from half of Isfahan, into your purse? Did we not advance you in an extraordinary way? Was it fitting that, in return for all these favours from us, you appropriated the water and property of whomever you could, to increase the area of sown ground for yourself? Did you not irrigate it, but to drive up prices, you also directed water into the sewers [wasting it], lest the area for which you were responsible should – God forbid – be fruitful, and crop prices should fall?"

"You raise two objections," he replied. "As for the first, in the year you refer to, I paid compensation for the damage to the crops. I submitted my resignation several times, but His Highness always refused. As regards the second, I did whatever I wanted to do. We had two or three years of drought. But I swear on the blessed head of His Highness, I did not earn a cent by way of dues for this! So how am I to blame?"

The Voice said, "What was the cause of grain hoarding and high prices? At a time when, in the normal course of affairs, bread would become cheap, why did you make threats and punish the bakers? What could the wretched poor do, and the unfortunate doorman and tradesman who had neither land nor reserves? You had the power to determine the rise and fall of prices at their origin,

ابا و استنکاف شدیدی ظاهراً کرده ولی از آنجائی که قلباً مایل بودند، میرزا فتحعلی خان ایشان را برده به حضور رسانید.

جناب ملاباشی میرزا احمد منجم باشی را به پای میزان حساب طلبیدند.

خطاب رسید: زمانی را که استطاعت نداشتی و دارای هیچ چیز نبودی، تقویم خطی نوشته به طهران می بردی و از ارکان به این وسیله بند می شدی نظرت هست؟ با قوز پشت گردن و زبان چون کوبیده در دهن تبسمی کرده گفت.

جواب: چه طوری؟

خطاب آمد: با این احمقی که داشتی و هیکل عجیبی که تشکیل داده بودی دولتت ندادیم، ملکت مرحمت نکردیم، عزتت عطا نفرمودیم، اجزای کل دیوان خانه اصفهانت نکردیم، مداخل ظل السلطان که نصف اصفهان را شامل بود در جیب تو داخل نکردیم ترقی فوق العاده به تو لطف نفرمودیم؟ در عوض این نعمتهای ما آیا سزاوار بود که آب و املاک هر کس را که بتوانی محض ازدیاد کشت با اراضی سپرده بخود ببری مشروب نمائی و محض تسعیر و گرانی جنس، آب را هم در هرزاب گذاری که املاک زیر دست مبادا کشت شود و قیمت جنس تنزل نماید.

جواب: این حرفهای شوما دوتاست یکی اینش اینکه من در سال مبلغی ضرر جنس را دادم. چند دفعه هم استعفاء دادم حضرت والا قبول نیمی کونند. یکی دیگر هم اینکه من هرچه اینشا این را کردم این دو سه سالۀ خشک سالی بسر مبارک حضرت والا یک دینار از وجه اجازه اینشا این نیمی کونند. تقصیر من چیست؟

خطاب: انبار غله و احتکار برای چه بود؟ وقتی که بالطبع نان میخواست ارزان شود تو سبب تهدید و تنبیه نانواها برای چه شدی؟ پس فقرای بیچاره و کسبه و نوکر باب بدبخت که ملک و انباری ندارند چه کنند؟ خود شما که رشتۀ ارزانی و گرانی اجناس دستتان است

and you did nothing! Even when, in the course of things, prices were about to fall, you did not lower your prices. You were content to let the grain go to dust in the storehouse, and sell at the high price you wanted. The basis of your income came from the high prices of bread and meat, which are the foundations of life for the poor."

"There is no god but God," he recited. "Whatever I wanted, they prevented. Oh, oh! Some things that were never spoken are spoken of here."

The Voice said, "These are just excuses. O watchmen, punish him for his actions. This cruel and vicious man should be punished for what he has done."

With profound dismay he cried, "How am I to blame? They have already recorded all these things about me, and now I am supposed to answer that I did this or that thing."

The Voice said, "We are ashamed of your behaviour. We questioned you. You were both the agent of oppression and choking off the daily sustenance of the people, and also the leader of tyranny, oppression and extortion. Your sins must be severely punished. Whatever you have tried to achieve has been in vain." Then God's agents did as they were bid.

Seeing no way out, he cried, "O Karim, go to my private apartments and say I've gone away. If any of my subjects continue to bring any things, take charge of them, but if they come to raise some issue, tell them to bugger off."

They led Mirzâ Hoseyn-'Ali Khan Kâshâni to the scales of justice.

The Voice said, "We are ashamed to reprove someone like you. There were taxes on the common people, which the government had abolished and which did not appear on any register, yet you exacted them on all the everyday food and necessities of the population and on the helpless poor, even taking much more. How much are the taxes on the city quarters? The tax on coal, on vegetables and the other taxes…? But as for the charges levied for bringing the necessities of ordinary people into the city, where are

اقدامی نمی کنید. بالطبع هم که می خواهد ارزان شود نمی گذارید. راضی دارید گندمها در انبار خاک شود و بقیمت مقصود بفروشید. عمدهٔ مداخل خود را از ممر گرانی نان و گوشت که مایهٔ زندگانی فقراست می نمائید.

جواب: لا اله الا الله من هر چه میخواهم اینشا این بوکونم نیمی گذارند. ای وای بعضی حرفها را که نمیشد بزنی عجب اینجا.

خطاب: اینها همه عذر است، ای مستحفظین کیفر اخلاق، این بیرحم موذی را به سزای خود برسانید.

جواب (با نهایت اضطراب: من چه تقصیری دارم؟ از بابت تمام اینها از من سند گرفته بودند حالا من باید جوابش را پس بدهم من اینشا این کردم.

خطاب: سوء رفتارهای تو را ما شرم داریم مؤاخذه نمائیم. هم مباشر ظلم و تنگی ارزاق مخلوق بودی هم راهنمای تعدی و اجحاف و سختی شدی، جزایت جز سختی و شداید نیست. جناب ملاباشی آنچه خواستند اینشا این بکنند نشد مأمورین به مأموریت خود رفتار کردند

لاعلاج صدا زدند: اهی کریم برو آنجا دم اندرون منهم رفتم اگر هم رعیتها چیزی آوردند بده تو اندرون اما اگر کاری داشتند اینشا این کون برند

میرزا حسینعلی خان کاشی را پای میزان حاضر کردند

خطاب رسید: خود شرم داریم که از مثل توئی مؤاخذه نمائیم که چرا مالیات عمومی را که دولت بخشیده و هیچ در کتابچهٔ دولت نیست تو از بارهائیکه قوت یومیه و لازمهٔ گذران هر روزه مردم و فقرای بینواست چندین برابر می گیری، مالیات خانات مگر چند است؟ مالیات ذغال، مالیات سبزی، مالیات سایر... و واردات اشیاء مایحتاج عامه که به شهر می آید مگر چه اندازه

these recorded in government records? Any one of your officials could levy these charges, to the extent of oppression, cruelty and excess.

"Do you remember what you were? Do you recall your childhood and the time you had your own trade? You wanted riches, and we have granted them to you. You wanted unlimited reverence and a high position, and we did not hold back one atom. Why this insistence on harassing the common people and putting the squeeze on profits deriving from the necessities of the masses?"

"O God," he replied. "I keep a closer eye on my own spending than others do. In the whole time I was in Isfahan, I paid no attention to progress in my own affairs. I have no great wealth, or great attachment to it. I admit, if there was no Zell-el-Soltân, there would be no Isfahan. I joined the hunt, and I got something for myself, thinking, who cares about Isfahan, and Zell-al-Soltân?"

The Herald cried, "It's true! It's true what they say:

> The dog from Kashan is better than the notables of Qom,
> Yet a dog is worth more than a man from Kashan.

The Voice said, "Administer the punishment for treason, for he has served neither his master nor the well-being of his fellow-creatures."

They dragged him away by force to the place where he belonged.

The Voice said, "Summon Mirzâ Bâqer Khan, the Chief Secretary of the government in Isfahan." His Excellency, the Chief Secretary, came and a crowd followed him.

The Voice said, "We want Mirzâ Bâqer Khan, the Chief Secretary! Who are these people?"

The Inquisitor for the Plain of Assembly replied, "My God, these are the Khans of Nâ'in, near Isfahan. They are inseparable. Whether you send them to hell or to paradise, they will go together."

در کتابچه دولت است که هر یک گماشتگان تو به نوعی اجحاف و تعدی و زیادتی می نمایند.

میدانی تو که بودی؟ زمان طفولیت و کسب شخصی خود را بخاطر داری؟ دولت می خواستی که برای تو فراهم کردیم. احترام و مکنت تمنا داشتی که ذره‌های فروگذار نکردیم. دیگر این اصرار در ایذای عامه و اجحاف در ازدیاد مالیات اشیاء مایحتاج عموم چرا؟

جواب: الهی من خود بیش از سایرین ملاحظه صرفه خود را می نمایم. هر زمان که در اصفهان تکلیف پیشرفت کار خود را نیابم نه ملکی زیاد دارم نه علاقه بسیار، گیرم ظل السلطان نبود و گمان می کنم اصفهانی خلق نشده بود. شکاری آمد کردم و دخلی رسید بردم، اصفهان کجاست و ظل السلطان کیست؟

منادی ندا در داد آری آری:

سگ کاشی به از اکابر قم
با وجودیکه سگ به از کاشی است

خطاب رسید: جزای خائن را بدهید که نه در صدد خدمت آقای خود، نه در خیال راحت خلق است.

کشان کشان بردندش و به مقام خود رساندندش.

خطاب رسید: میرزا باقرخان منشی باشی اصفهان را حاضر کنید.

جناب منشی باشی می آمد، جمعی دنبال ایشان بودند.

خطاب آمد: ما میرزا باقر خان منشی باشی را خواستیم این گروه کیستند؟

مفتش صحرای محشر عرض کرد: الهی خوانین نائینند که جزء لایتجزای یکدیگر هستند. اگر امر به دوزخ فرمائی با هم اند و هر گاه حکم به بهشت نمائی توأمند.

The Voice said, "Bâqer Khan, do you remember how you began, and the distressed condition of yourself and your father? How many favours we bestowed upon you! How often we have been merciful in your case! Are you aware of this?" As embarrassed and confused people do, he fixed his eyes on the ground, bowing and scraping, his mouth full of flattery, and finally replied in the same style, "Truly, I accept my place as your servant and devotee, and I have never forgotten the priceless divine favours." He went so far in flattery, and bowing low and praising God, that words cannot describe or explain it.

The Voice said, "We assign no blame and bring no charges. We are obliged to have compassion on you and praise you in full, in light of the firm faith of your house, and its hereditary nobility. But why did you make yourself a willing instrument for Zell-al-Soltân's political schemes? At one time you closed your eyes to the rights of the innocent oppressed, at another you wrote a death sentence for a modest person. One minute you were failing to implement the law, the next you were acting to spread corruption. Why did you participate in writing letters to stir up trouble? Why did you circulate hostile pamphlets? And during all the months and years in which you were an indispensable participant in this administration, did you not see and understand how extensive was the mistreatment of the ordinary people, how persistently severe punishments were administered? Did you learn nothing from the outcome of the affair of Sârem-al-Dowle? Have you not seen the end of Moshir-al-Molk? Were you not a participant at the end of Ebrâhim Khalil Khan?"

Suddenly I saw Sheykh Sa'di of Shiraz, that poet of erect stature and mellifluous tones. He arose and began to recite:

> One day in the bathhouse a dear one passed to me
> a lump of finely perfumed clay.

خطاب: باقر خان حال اولت و پریشانی خود و پدرت را خاطر داری، چه نعمتها که به تو دادیم، چه مرحمتها که در حق تو کردیم آیا قدر میدانی و به خاطر می آوری؟ مثل اشخاص بسیار شرمنده و خجل چشم بزمین دوخته متصل تعظیم می کند و تعارف می نماید. با آن وضع و حال عرض می کند:

جواب: واقعاً مراتب بندگی و فدویت خود را داشته و از الطاف بیکران الهیت هیچ فراموش نکرده ام.

به اندازه ای تعارف نمود و سجده کرد و تسبیح تمجید نمود که به توصیف و تعریف نمی گنجد.

خطاب: ما اغماض نمی نمائیم و ایراد نمی گیریم. در اعتقاد و تدین طایفه گی و نجابت ارثی شماها نسبتاً واجب الرحم، کامل التفضل هستید. ولی جهت چیست که تو خود را آلت اجرای پولیتیک ظل السلطان کرده گاهی اغماض از حق مظلومی می کنی، گاهی رقم در ریختن خونمحجوبی می نویسی، ساعتی اهمال در اجرای حقی می نمائی، زمانی افساد مسئله‌ای را محرک می شوی، برای چه داخل کار در نوشتجات عنادآمیز می گردی؟ نگر تو در این چند مدت و سال در امورات و کارهای این اداره داخل و مستحضر بودی ندیدی و نفهمیدی که ایذای عامه در این اقدامات و مؤاخذات شدیده در این اصرارات است. آخر کار صارم الدوله را نفهمیدی؟ عاقبت مشیر الملک را ندیدی؟ واقعه ابراهیم خلیل خان را مستحضر نشدی!

شیخ سعدی را ناگهان دیدم قدی راست و نطقی آراسته و فریاد زد:

گلی خوشبوی در حمام روزی
رسید از دست محبوبب به دستم

I asked that clay, "are you ambergris, or musk?
  Your enchanting perfume has made me drunk."
The clay responded, "I'm worthless clay.
  I spent some time beside a rose.
My friend's perfection passed to me,
  If not, I'd be the earth I am."

Mirzâ Bâqer Khan searched his mind for an adequate answer, but feeling pressed for time, and by anxieties, he could not find a suitable rejoinder to this speech. As an aid to thinking, he pinched his nostrils between two fingers. Then he rubbed his fingers together, and cleared his throat repeatedly. Without being aware of it, he was constantly rubbing his hands together, as if washing them. After hearing what Saʿdi recited, he looked shamefaced. Agitated, and full of anxiety about his fate, he kept his eyes on the ground as was his habit in conversation. Then he raised his eyes and looked at the Sheykh with an engaging smile. He spread his hands in a gesture to Saʿdi, and said,

"God, the truth always comes out. The Sheykh speaks the truth. From the beginning of my service in Isfahan, His Highness called my father 'Imam Zeyn-al-Âbedin the sick' because he looked so oppressed and undernourished. I too served the late Moshir-al-Molk and then entered the service of His Highness, in the same position as my father. I had no power, in fact, no authority at all: I was an outsider, taking no initiatives. While I had a role in some oppressive acts and participated in some injustices, I said to myself, 'I take refuge in God, I will never instigate such things. I will never join in, to the detriment of Muslims, and I certainly will never in my life take anyone's property.'

"But I was younger then, and the piety and virtue of the young are also immature. Little by little, I became associated with the entourage and household servants of His Sacred Highness, I became less conscious of the reprehensibility of certain demands, and so, imperceptibly, I became what I am. I play and dance better than my teacher. This is the story of the change in me, it explains my present condition.

بدو گفتم که مشگی یا عبیری
که از بوی دلاویز تو مستم
بگفتا من گلی ناچیز بودم
ولیکن مدتی با گل نشستم
کمال همنشین در من اثر کرد
وگرنه من همان خاکم که هستم

خان میرزا باقرخان که در تفکر و تعقل خود با کمال عجله و نهایت اضطراب گردش و کوشش میکرد که شاید جوابی کافی و عرضی وافی یافت نماید و در هر سوراخ و ثقبهٔ مغز خود سری فرو برده بود و چیزی پیدا نکرده بود که قابل جواب این خطاب باشد و از ازدیاد فکر با دو انگشت آن به آن دو لولهٔ بینی را فشار داده بعد انگشتان را به هم می مالید و گاهگاهی سینه و راه خرخره را صاف میکرد دقیقه بدقیقه بلا اراده دو دست را (بطوریکه در شست و شو بهم می مالند) بهم می مالید بعد از استماع این نطق شیخ سعدی نظر محجوبانه و (پر اضطراب خود را که اغلب در مذاکرات عادت شده) بزمین انداخته بود، بالا کرده نگاهی با تبسم شیرینی بشیخ انداخته با دو دست اشاره به سعدی و عرض کرد: الهی شاهد از غیب هم می رسد. جناب شیخ درست میفرماید. از ابتدای نوکریم به اصفهان حضرت والا اسم پدرم را امام زین العابدین بیمار گذارده بود، از بسکه ظاهر مظلوم و نحیفی داشت. خود من هم در دستگاه مرحوم مشیرالملک و بعد در استخدام حضرت والا با حالت خست پدر بزرگوارم دارای هیچ مکنت و دولتی نبوده و خیلی هم بی دست و پا و محجوب و بیخیال بودم. خیال بعضی تعدیات یا شرکت در بعضی اجحافات را هم که می کردم پیش خودم می گفتم العیاذ بالله هرگز این حالات از من ناشی نخواهد شد. ابداً در ایذای مسلمی شرکت نخواهم نمود و یقیناً در تمامی عمر به ملک کسی دست اندازی نمی نمایم. ولی آن ایام جوانتر بودم، تدین و حقشناسی جوان هم جوان است. کم کم با اجزاء و چاکران حضور حضرت اقدس والا محشور شده قبح بعضی مطالب از صفحهٔ ضمیرم برداشته شد و یواش یواش این شده ام که از استادم بهتر می زنم و از معلمم خوبتر می رقصم. این است شرح حرکات من و چنین است توضیح حالات من.

"Lord, deal with us according to your grace, and not according to your justice."

The Voice said, "What did you do about the petitions of the oppressed, or to satisfy the cases of people's rights that were your own responsibility? Did you do anything? Did you implement any right for anyone?"

"I will do it all tomorrow," he replied, "and definitely I will do it tomorrow."

A group of people raised a cry of lamentation, wailing, "O God, this is the day after the resurrection, and even now the Chief Secretary's promise has not been fulfilled."

The Voice said, "Mirzâ Bâqer Khan, we will extend our grace and mercy to you, according to the promise, if you keep your word and fulfil your duties to our creatures." This was agreed, and the next day, the cases of all those wronged, and of the petitioners, were taken care of, and their sufferings were public knowledge, so that the station of the Chief Secretary [in heaven] could be determined.

The Voice said, "Summon Mirzâ Asadollâh Khan, the Vazir." In the far distance, across this boundless plain, I saw his Excellency the Vazir, short in stature but wearing a tall hat and voluminous robes. He lurched towards us, and arrived looking worried, very bewildered, indeed terrified; his disturbed condition was so evident in his face that all those present on the Plain of Assembly believed that his misdeeds were perhaps more numerous than those of others, and the heinousness of his conduct greater than is usual, among all ranks of society. First he asked where His Highness, the Prince, might be. Then he enquired what had happened to Rokn-al-Molk and the Mollâbâshi. He asked one person the reason for his summons, and another the reason for this urgency and the purpose of the interrogation.

The Voice said, "If you bring this individual a few steps further, he will perish. Despite all his bad deeds, he also had some virtues. Sometimes he helped the poor and his own relatives.

ربنا عاملنا بفضلک و لاتعاملنا بعد لک.
خطاب: عرایض مظلومین و اتمام امور حقهٔ مرجوعه به خود را چه کردی؟ آیا انجام دادی کاری را؟ و به اتمام رسانیدی حقی را؟
جواب: فردا تمام کرده به عرض می رسانم و حتماً فردا انجام می دهم.
صدای فریاد جمعی بلند شد که خدایا امروز فردای قیامت است و هنوز منشی باشی موعدش نرسیده.
خطاب رسید: میرزا باقر خان، در بارهٔ تو به فضل و ترحم وعده می کنیم اگر تو نیز به عهد خود با بندگان وفا نمائی.
قرار شد فردا تمام متظلمین و عارضین کارشان انجام پذیرد و تکلیفشان معلوم گردد تا تعیین مقام منشی باشی هم مشخص شود.
خطاب آمد: میرزا اسدالله خان وزیر را حاضر نمائید.
از دور دست این صحرای نامتناهی دیدم جناب وزیر با قدی کوتاه و کلاهی بلند و لبادهٔ گشاده می غلتید و می آمد با حالتی خیلی مضطرب و حواسی خیلی متوحش. بنوعی حالت وحشت و انقلاب از چهره اش پیدا و هویدا بود که تمام اهل محشر گمان کردند شاید سوء اعمال او بیش از تمام و قبح اخلاق او زیاده از اجزای خاص و عام است. گاهی از این مستفسر می شد که حضرت والا کجا هستند؟ شرحی به آن اظهار می کرد که جناب رکن الملک و ملاباشی چه شدند؟ از یکی می پرسیدند که سبب احضار چیست؟ از دیگری سئوال می کرد که علت عجله و استنطاق کدامست؟
خطاب رسید: این شخص را اگر چند قدم بیشتر بیاورید هلاک خواهد شد. با آنهمه سوء رفتار بعضی اخلاق هم داشت که گاهی دستگیری به فقرا و اقوام خود می نمود.

He was not greedy or seeking his own benefit. Leave him in peace and raise no objections. This poor fellow is content with the bare necessities of life."

One or two of his friends and some women from the Shah-Shahan quarter followed Mirzâ Assadolah Khan, pursuing pleasure and merrymaking, vanishing from sight.

The Voice was then addressed to the summoning chamberlains, saying, "Why have you not led Seyyed Ja'far Bid-Âbâdi before the court? Was he not among the clerics, did he not consider himself to be in the rank of *mojtaheds*? Ensure he appears here quickly because his response to the accusations made by a number of souls on the Plain of Assembly is eagerly awaited." Half an hour passed, and a terrifying voice came from the throne of God, demanding, "Where is this Seyyed Ja'far?"

One or two of those instructed to summon that gentleman replied, "Lord, we went there. He is spending some time in his private quarters."

The Voice said, "Go and bring this arrogant Seyyed by force." To cut a long story short, some officials and angels set off. Gabriel was in the lead, Israfil was his assistant and Michael was his Herald, and bringing up the rear came Ezra'il with the guardian angels of hell to assist. Half an hour or more had passed when I saw that excellent gentleman appearing on one side of the Plain of Assembly. He was riding a little black donkey, with his cape over his head. Seyyed Abu Tâlib was running in front of the donkey. The hapless Mirzâ Rezâ, his secretary, followed, as unobtrusively as a shadow in the shadows. The donkey arrived, and stood before the scales of justice. The Crier announced:

> The donkey who went to get thistles has come,
> the other donkeys have a gleam in their eyes.

That gentleman did not get off the donkey. He showed some signs of weakness and lethargy, pretending to be on the point of death. Seyyed Abu Talib was in league with his charlatanism. Cries of "Sir,

حرص و اندوخته حاصل ننمود، رهایش نمایند و ایرادی وارد ننمایند. این بیچاره فقط به عیش و نوشی قانع است.
یکی دو از رفقا و بعضی مخدرات محلهٔ شهشهان هم بدنبالش افتادند و دنبال حال و نشاه خود روان شده از نظر غایب شدند.
خطاب به فراشان آمد که: سید جعفر بیدآبادی را چرا حاضر نکرده اید؟ مگر در جزو علما نبود و در سلک مجتهدین خود را داخل نمی نمود؟ زود حاضرش سازید و فوراً ظاهرش نمائید که مؤاخذات اعمال جمعی از اهالی محشر را منتظر داشته. یک نیم ساعتی طول کشیده، تهدید از بارگاه تعالی آمد که: چه شد این سید جعفر؟
یکی دو از مأمورین احضار آقا عرض کردند: الهی رفتیم، در درون تشریف داشتند.
خطاب رسید: بروید بیاورید این سید متفرعن را.
بالجمله چندین مامور و ملک رفتند، جبرئیل روانه شد، اسرافیل مامور شد، میکائیل فرستاده شد تا بالاخره عزرائیل با مالک دوزخ مامور شد. دو سه ربعی طول نکشید دیدم جناب مستطاب آقا از گوشهٔ صحرای محشر پیدا شدند. سوار بر الاغی کوچک و کبود، پوستین را بر سر کشیده، آقا سید ابوطالب هم جلو الاغ می دود. بیچاره میرزا رضای محرر در دنبال آقا، سیاهی به سیاهی آهسته روان بود. الاغ آمد دم میزان حساب ایستاد. منادی ندا در داد:

آمد آن خر که رفته بود گون
چشم خرهای دیگری روشن

آقا از خر پیاده نشدند. مقداری اظهار کسالت و نقاهت و مرده بازی درآوردند. آقا سید ابوطالب مشغول شارلاتانی شد. آقا

Sir" were filling the air at the base of the scales of justice, but Seyyed Abu Tâlib pushed the people back a little and said, "What's the fuss? Do you think this is a show? This is his Honour, not some demon of the desert."

The Voice said, "Do you have something of merit, as provision for your journey and to win our favour? What service have you rendered?"

"I'm a little deaf, speak louder!"

"Seyyed Ja'far, did we not make you the son of Seyyed Mohammed Bâqer? Did we not give you the post of supreme ecclesiastical dignitary, in spite of an unfortunate pallid face and a crooked body that attracts disdain? Did we not grant you leadership in the religious community? Did we not give you the respect and admiration of the mass of the faithful? Despite your lack of knowledge and your lack of learning, did we not raise you to a prominent place in the mosque and as a preacher? Yet is there any crime or ugly vice you have left untouched? You spent your whole time protecting the crooks and riff-raff in the Bidâbâd quarter – the ruffians and fugitives from justice. Is there any crime they did not commit at your instigation? Was there any house where lives and property were safe from them, because of you? You were the co-conspirator of every extortionate official and the associate of every outlaw. Why did you confiscate the property of Prince Jalâli, at Dehak, which should have passed to your nephew Seyyed Mohammad Bâqer? Why did you seize charitable trusts meant for widows and the needy? Why did you appropriate the fiefdom over the village of Zafreh, which should have passed to Soltân Hoseyn Mirzâ, the old prince?

"O Seyyed Ja'far, if we were to individually list the estates you appropriated, and your acts of oppression, you would be standing before the scales of justice for several years to hear them. You gave Hâjji Sâni Beyk, the superintendent of properties, such a free hand to commit injustices that all hands were raised to us in protest, and the more crimes he committed, the more respect you gave him!"

آقا دورۀ میزان را پر کرده. قدری سید ابوطالب مردم را پس و پیش می کند و می گوید: چه خبر است، چه تماشائی دارد؟ آقاست، غول بیابانی که نیست!

خطاب رسید: برای توشۀ خود و رضایت خاطر ما چه ثوابی آورده ای، چه عبادتی کرده ای؟

جواب: من گوشم قدری سنگین شده، بلندتر بفرمائید.

خطاب: سید جعفر، تو را پسر حاجی سید محمد باقر نکردیم با این رؤیت منحوس و پیس و فطرت مذموم و خبیث، آیا ریاست ملی به تو ندادیم؟ در عموم عامه آیا محترم و معززت ننمودیم؟ با عدم دانش و علم آیا صاحب مسجد و محراب و مسندت نکردیم؟ اما از کار های ذمیمه و اخلاق قبیحه چه بود که نداشتی؟ دائماً حامی اشرار و اراذل محلۀ بیدآباد از لران و پاچه ورمالدیگان می شدی. آیا چه ایذائی که به پشتگرمی تو نمی کردند؟ خانه ای نبود که از دست آنان به سبب واهمۀ مال و جان راحت داشته باشند. با هر متصدی هم رأی بودی و با هر متخطی همراه می شدی! ملک (دهک) شاهزاده جلالی را که راجع به سید محمد باقر پسر برادرت بود چرا ضبط کردی؟ امانات بیوه زنان و بیچارگان را چرا غصب نمودی؟ ملک زفره که تیول و راجع به سلطان حسین میرزای پیره شاهزاده بود چرا گرفتی؟ ای سید جعفر اراضی که غصب نمودی و تعدیاتی که کردی که بخواهم یک یک بیان کنم چندین سال باید در پای میزان بایستی و گوش دهی. دست تعدی حاجی ثانی بیک مباشر املاک را به اندازه ای دراز کرده بودی که دستی نبود که از دستش به درگاه ما دراز نباشد و هر چه بیشتر او ایذا می کرد تو بیشتر احترامش می گذاردی.

His Eminence turned to the Angel of the Voice and asked, "What is the source of these messages? Who had the courage to voice these accusations?"

"God, the Creator, the framer of all creatures," said the angel.

"Could you speak up, and more clearly? I wasn't paying attention."

"Your God, your Creator, your Lord," said the angel.

His Eminence thought, meditated and said, "I swear by the blessed dust of the late Hojjat al-Islam [my father], I do not know him."

"Jafar! What temerity is this?" asked the angel. "Is this the way for you to speak? It is His Majesty and his power that has raised all these creatures. This is the place where He hears accusations and renders judgement. What is this denial? Where are you getting this from?"

"Could you repeat his name?"

"The Lord of the worlds, Creator of all beings and the whole world."

"I will pour wine on the grave of the late Hojjat al-Islam, I have racked my brain and I do not remember any such name. I know nothing about it. I know him not." He turned to Mirzâ Rezâ, his secretary, and told him, "Look closely in your register and lists, to be certain whether anything like this name is listed."

With extreme vehemence and anger, the Blessed Voice addressed the stewards of the Day of Judgement, saying, "Throw this contemptible Seyyed in our sea of fire. Carry this accursed fellow to the hottest regions of hell."

The custodians of hell came to take him with chains made of fire and flaming cudgels. But he did not get off his donkey. He said, "I swear by the late Hojjat al-Islam that I will not move a step, under any circumstances."

The custodians replied, "Excuse us, but this is not Isfahan! It is not a place where you can plead, or shut your eyes in anger, or take off your coat and go to your private quarters."

جناب آقا رو کردند به ملک خطاب آورنده که این پیغامات را که داده و مؤاخذات را که جرئت مذاکره نموده؟

ملک گفت: حضرت پروردگاری خالق موجودات، خدا و باری.

جناب آقا: بلندتر و واضحتر بگو ملتفت نشدم.

ملک: خدای تو خالق تو پروردگار تو!

جناب آقا فکری کرده، تأملی فرموده گفتند: به ارواح خاک مرحوم حجت الاسلام ابداً نمی شناسمشان.

ملک: یا جعفر این چه جسارتی است، این چه عبارتست. عظمت و قدرت اوست که تمام موجودات را فرا گرفته، این مقام مؤاخذه و انتشار عدالت اوست. این انکار چیست، این اظهار کدام است؟

جناب آقا: مکر بفرمائید اسمشان را.

ملک: خدای عالمیان خالق موجودات و جهان.

جناب آقا: به قبر مرحوم حجت الاسلام شراب ریخته ام که آنچه فکر می کنم هیچ همچو اسمائی به خاطرم نمی آید اصلاً شناسائی ندارم، ابداً نمی شناسم.

بعد رو کردند به میرزا رضای محرر، امر فرمودند که میرزا، شما در کتابچه و ثبتهای خود خوب ملاحظه و رسیدگی کنید که آیا چنین اسمی در آنجاها یافت می شود؟

خطاب مستطاب با نهایت شدت و غضب به مامورین روز جزا رسید که: بکشید این سید مردود را در دریای آتش ما. ببرید این ملعون را در دوزخ شدید و سخط ما.

ریختند عمله جات با زنجیرهای آتشین و عمودهای مشتعل که او را ببرند، آقا از خر پیاده نمی شدند.

جناب آقا: به ارواح خاک مرحوم حجت الاسلام اگر قدم از قدم بردارم. به هیچوجه نخواهم آمد!

مامورین گفتند: ببخشید، اینجا اصفهان نیست که ناز نمائید، قهر کنید، پوستین را اول داده به اندرون بدوید.

They pulled him down by force. They had taken him only a few steps when he turned to the ruffians, the blackguards and the street toughs from among the traders and inhabitants of Bid-Âbâd, and said, "Hey, you cowards! Will you just stand there, while they drag me off in this shameful way?"

All of a sudden, I saw a group of them take up their hawker's boards, clubs and the beams of their scales. Bent on mischief, they attacked the custodians of hell mercilessly. In fact, they were beating anyone they came across.

I turned away to escape this crowd, when a club struck the side of my head. My head felt wet; I was bleeding. The pain and fear woke me, and I saw I was bathed in sweat. I saw it was some hours into the night. The dream's extreme horror had left me stupefied, my body trembling to such an extent that I was rooted to my bed, unable to move. Truly, this long dream, lasting several hours, had openly revealed to me the majestic affairs of the spiritual realm.

I heard that someone was knocking on the door of my house. The servant who was on duty came in and told me that it was a certain long-time friend and confidant of mine, whom I love, and whose guest I had been. I gave a sign to invite him in. He came in and saw me, agitated and helpless in bed, and became upset and frightened himself. The sight of him fortified me to some extent. Weak as I was, I said, "My dear brother, don't be alarmed. My extraordinary condition is due to a remarkable dream."

"Tell it to me," he said.

I raised myself in my bed, and told him my story, over the course of several hours.

He said, "What a remarkable dream! It is a commentary on some familiar events. It doesn't seem at all exaggerated or extreme. But my friend, you should never recount it to anyone, or explain it, or reveal its particulars and context. People will think that you intend to expose and protest the ugliness of their actions. They will harm you and make things hard for you."

I said, "If I did not believe in the events of the resurrection

جبراً کشیدند. چند قدمی که ایشان را بردند، جناب آقا رو کردند به لران و مشدیان و الواطان از کسبه و ساکنین بیدآباد، گفتند: آهای بی غیرتها ایستاده اید و مرا به این افتضاح می برند.

که یکدفعه دیدم جمعیتی از آنها دست به تختهٔ دکان و چماق و چوب قپان کرده هر یک عربده جویان حمله به عمله جات دوزخ کرده بی محابا به هر کس می رسیدند، می زدند.

من تا خواستم از میان این جمعیت رو به فرار نهم، چماقی به گوشهٔ سرم خورده سر دهن باز کرد خون جاری شد. از شدت درد و وحشت از خواب بیدار شدم، خود را غرق در عرق دیدم. از روز چند ساعتی برآمده بود. از شدت وحشت این خواب لرزه باندامم افتاده بود. مات و مبهوت از لرزش اعصاب در رختخواب قوهٔ حرکت نداشتم. واقعاً این خواب طولانی در این چند ساعت مراتب عظمت عالم روحانی را معلوم می دارد و مکشوف می کند.

شنیدم که در می زنند و به شدت می کوبند. مستخدمه ای که آنجا بود آمد گفت: آقا فلان رفیق است و آن مونس و شفیق که همیشه انیس او بودی و جلیس او می شدی. اشاره کردم تشریف بیاورند. آمد مرا در رختخواب افتاده و پریشان دید، مضطرب و هراسان شد. دیدار او قدری تقویت به وجودم داد. با ضعف و کمال نحف گفتم: برادر جان توحش مدار که تغییر حالت من از رؤیای عجیبی است که دیده ام.

گفت: چیست؟

برخاستم در رختخواب نشستم. چند ساعتی طول کشید تا برایش نقل کردم.

گفت: عجب خوابی است که تعبیرش مقارن واقع است و ابداً اغراق و بیهوده بینی نبوده ولی عزیز من مبادا این خواب را به کسی نقل و بیان کنی و تفصیل و عنوان نمائی که گمان می کنند مقصودت ایراد و انکشاف قبایح اعمال آنها بوده اذیتت می کنند، صدمه ات می زنند.

گفتم: فلانی اگر یقینی در مراتب حشر و عوالم نشر نداشتم و دلیل می خواستم،

and judgement, and wanted proof, this dream in itself is reliable evidence and a vivid miracle of proof.[73] Given such certainty, how could I not explain about the spiritual worlds, but conceal them? Perhaps it was intended to bring ease to a people. Serenity for many might be concealed in this dream!"

"What advantage is there in disclosing it? What will be the results of recounting and explaining it? The people of Isfahan know these people, in fact they know such people by the hundreds. And we cannot consider the rich and powerful of Iran to be ignorant of these things. But government officials and people living in other countries, they may suspect you are exaggerating, and make fun."

"My dear brother," I replied, "the foreigners know our doings and behaviour better than we know ourselves. They see every corner, every dust mote, better than we do. It is we who are uninformed and cowardly. In any case, I decided this very week to take my whole household to another city, and settle in a pleasant house. As for my property and belongings, I will sell some and part with the remainder cheaply, offering them to various people."

He said, "I too intend to visit the shrine of a saint, so we can travel together as far as Tehran."

So saying, he took the book containing the collected works of Sa'di from its niche and opened it. The book fell open at this poem, through which the eyes of affection and humane understanding shine:

No man is e'er made noble, but by his soul's humanity,
fine clothes are not a sign of humanity.

Even if he seem a man, with mouth and ears and nose,
He's just an image on the wall, but for his humanity.

Lust and anger, eating and sleeping, lead to ignorance and darkness. An animal knows nothing of humanity.

Be a man in truth, for truly, I know birds
Who can speak the language of humanity.

این خواب خود مستندی معتبر و معجزه ای مجسم است. با اینحالت یقین چگونه تلقینات عوالم روحانی را بیان ننمایم و کتمان کنم. شاید راحت خلقی در آن منظور نظر باشد و استراحت جمعی در این مستور.

گفت: چه فایده در نشر آن و ثمری در ذکر و بیان آن است؟ ساکنین اصفهان که به عینه بلکه صد چندان این اشخاص نگرانند، اکابر و اعیان داخله هم که بیخبرشان نمی شود گفت. مأمورین و ساکنین خارجه هم که ممکن است گمان اغراق برند و با تمسخر و تمضحک عنوان نمایند.

گفتم برادر عزیزم خارجی ها از اعمال و رفتار ما بهتر از خود ما مستحضر و گوشه گوشه و ذره ذره را خوبتر نگران و مخبرند، مائیم که بی خبران و بی همتان هستیم.

گذشته از آن من در این هفته عازم شده ام که عیال و خانمان را برداشته در شهری دیگر بروم و در مکانی پسندیده سکنی گیرم و ملک و علایق خود را هم بعضی را فروخته و باقی را هم به این و آن به قیمت کسر و نقصان واگذار و تسلیم خواهم کرد.

گفت: من هم به زیارت عازمم و تا طهران همراه هستم. در این ضمن کتاب کلیات سعدی را از طاقچه برداشته باز کرد، این غزل آمد و چشم محبت و انسانیت را روشن نمود:

تن آدمی شریف است به جان آدمیت

نه همین لباس زیباست نشان آدمیت

اگر آدمی به چشم است و زبان و گوش و بینی

چه میان نقش دیوار و میان آدمیت

خور و خواب و خشم و شهوت شغب است و جهل و ظلمت

حیوان خبر ندارد ز جهان آدمیت

به حقیقت آدمی باش وگرنه مرغ دانم

که همی سخن بگوید به زبان آدمیت

A man can achieve a station where nothing is seen but God
Behold how high is the limit to the station of humanity!

Was it not a man, Adam, who remained in the grasp of the Devil?
Indeed, angels have no access to the station of humanity.

If the brutal habit in your nature dies,
throughout your life you will live through the soul of humanity.

You see the flight of birds. Free yourself from the bonds of lust,
Come to that door, and see, the soaring of humanity.

Become a man through this advice, not through your self,
for Saʿdi too, heard from a man, the description of humanity.

رسد آدمی به جائی که به جز خدا نبیند
بنگر که تا حد است مکان آدمیت
مگر آدمی نبودی که اسیر دیو ماندی
که فرشته ره ندارد به مکان آدمیت
اگر این درنده خونی ز طبیعتت بمیرد
همه عمر زنده باشی به روان آدمیت
طیران مرغ دیدی، تو زپای بند شهوت
به درآی تا ببینی طیران آدمیت
به نصیحت آدمی شو نه به خویشتن که سعدی
هم از آدمی شنیده است بیان آدمیت

Appendix

The True Dream in Malekzâde's *History of the Iranian Constitutional Revolution*

A passage from *The True Dream* is cited by Malekzâde in his *History of the Iranian Constitutional Revolution*.[74] It is entirely devoted to God's questioning of Âqâ Sheykh Mohammad-Taqi Najafi. This is an important passage as it depicts several traits of Âqâ Najafi that are confirmed in other sources. Choubiné places this passage separately, as an addendum. In it, and in other passages of Malekzâde's voluminous *History*, Âqâ Najafi is depicted as a shallow man, an oppressor, despotic and intimidating. Malekzâde tells, for instance, how the rich Âqâ Najafi avoided paying taxes for several years. The Minister for the Economy, Mirzâ Asadollâh Khan, invites him to his house to arrange the payment. When Âqâ Najafi comes to the door, the Minister goes to him, kisses his hands and treats him with all possible respect. When the Minister offers him some cookies, Âqâ Najafi shamelessly says, "People talk about the Minister's ideas about religion." By this Âqâ Najafi implied that the Minister is accused of heresy and that the religious law did not permit him to eat anything in his house. The frightened Minister, who feared for his life, asked for paper and a pen and, with a pale face and shuddering body, wrote: "His Excellency the Ayatollah has paid all his tax debts on his estates and work to me. From now on, he has no unpaid accounts with the Ministry." On seeing the paper, Âqâ Najafi smiled and took one cookie, saying, "I consider the Minister more Muslim than any person and I do not doubt his interest in the principles of the holy religion."[75]

The following passage draws a very vivid picture of this fear-inspiring man. The passage starts as if it is the beginning of *The True Dream*, but it is not clear where the passage belongs in *The True Dream*.

> In a dream I saw the Plain of Resurrection, and Âqâ Sheykh Mohammad-Taqi, known as Âqâ Najafi, in his actual physical body, was brought to this plain, riding on a white donkey and accompanied by a group of clerics and ruffians, shouting prayers to the prophet.
>
> Âqâ Najafi looked around in bewilderment and asked one of the ulama who stood before his donkey, "What is happening?"

Suddenly the Voice issued from the Throne of Awe, saying, "O Sheykh Mohammad-Taqi! We placed you in the world with the rank of the Prophet's vicegerent. We entrusted our laws to your hands. We placed the happiness of Our servants, who are a divine gift, in your hands. We gave you knowledge, wealth, power, health, authority, persuasiveness, long life and everything that makes a man happy. We commanded you to implement the perspicuous pronouncement '*and judge fairly between the people.*'[76] Why did you deviate from the duties your Lord had stipulated and made obligatory for you? Why did you defy the divine decrees, turning away from the path of rectitude and truth? You trampled on truth and justice, which are the foundations and basis of the holy religion of Islam, choosing instead oppression and despotism. You spread disorder and hypocrisy, making God's people a plaything for your passions.

"We entrusted Islam to you, the Islam which, following the Prophet Mohammad (peace be upon him) and the true executor of his will ['Ali], had reached a zenith of glory and greatness, shining its lights to the east and west of the world, and whose firm foundations and clear laws had borne fruit in man's peaceful and ordered life, an Islam which had erected the mighty palace of piety, sincerity and knowledge of God and His Oneness. You ruined the firm foundations of this, the world's most comprehensive religion, for the sake of a few days of worldly pleasure and position, to appease your lower desires, placing the unbelievers' collar of servitude upon the neck of Muslims. You left Islam stricken by weakness and negligence, and you corrupted the character of the faithful. You wreaked havoc to such an extent that the followers of less worthy religions declared Islam a religion opposed to civilization and human progress, considering the holy Koran as a hindrance to achieving happiness and the [higher] levels of learning and knowledge.

"Why did you eschew the saying of the Prophet 'Seeking knowledge is a duty for all Muslims, male or female'?[77] Why did you consider obtaining learning and knowledge to be contrary to Islam? Why did you declare those who earnestly seek greater knowledge and piety to be unbelievers, and shut the doors of learning and knowledge to Muslims, exhorting the people to folly and a life in the darkness of ignorance?

"Why did you not heed the words of your Lord who says, 'take counsel with them in the affair' (Koran 3: 159), calling consultation in the important affairs of the government and the people a heretical innovation? Throughout your life, in ways such as these, you encouraged an arbitrary and tyrannical government, joining them in plundering and accumulating possessions. Why did you not follow the clear saying, 'God bids you to justice and fairness,'[78] instead taking the oppression of God's creatures as your occupation, and encouraging and assisting the injustice of tyrants?

"Why did you trample on 'seek knowledge even in China'?[79] Why did you declare those who journeyed with much hardship to advanced and developed countries to acquire knowledge and learning, and to return with a haul of learning and knowledge to their homeland, to be unbelievers and atheists?

"Why did you declare the supporters of freedom and justice to be materialists spreading corruption, whose blood might be shed? Why did you gather around yourself a number of trouble-makers, giving them the title of religious students, and plundering and pillaging God's creatures with their help? Why did you declare Seyyed Mârbini a heretic to confiscate his state, and shed the blood of this old, venerable and blameless son of the Prophet? Have you no shame before God or man?[80]

"Why did you declare the two ill-fated brothers, merchants who sought what you owed them, to be unbelievers and polytheists, and hand them over to be killed in a horrible manner?[81] Why did you pronounce the sentence of heresy on the tax officer, who in pursuance of his duties demanded the government taxes from you, but you wanted to assess the tax on your produce, which was thousands of donkey-loads, at the rate of five small silver coins per donkey-load? He refused and you declared him a heretic and atheist, and you killed this innocent poor man, leaving his family without protection.

"What justice and fairness was upheld when you entered into temporary marriages with virgin girls of ten to twelve years old, to satisfy your lusts? After enjoying that for a while, you left these ill-fated girls, creating hundreds of beggars and prostitutes.

"On what grounds did you forbid the study of divine philosophy, which is the foundation of development for the souls of men, declaring the sage philosophers to be heretics and atheists? Why did you pick up Rumi's spiritual poem *The Mathnavi*, which is one of Persia's glories, with tongs, and throw it outside, saying that its author had gone astray and followed no religion, and that the readers of this treasured poem are materialists and against Islam?

"What faith and religious law was upheld when you declared the new-style schools to be houses of Satan, and their founders faithless apostates? Why did you call the children who went to these schools for education impure and depraved? Why did you threaten their parents? Why did you give permission to shed the blood of the advocates of this holy institution, calling them faithless polytheists?

"Why did you use the Faith of God and the Prophet's decrees as a pretext for oppression and torment, using them to uproot civilization and humanity, with no fear of the day of Resurrection and the accounting? You had no shame before God or his Prophet, doing whatever you wanted."

Âqâ Najafi was shaken by the words of the Creator. Running his fingers through his bushy henna-dyed beard, he turned his face to those who surrounded him and said, "Turn the donkey's head towards the world. This person [referring to God] also has his saddle-bag awry. He has no faith or religion. He is repeating the very things that some heretics are saying in the world." But the minions of torment gave him no reprieve; they threw him headfirst into the nethermost depths of hell.

Here Malekzâde adds that the author of *The True Dream*, after depicting the deeds of the government officers and clerics, turns to the court of God, the beloved and just Creator, lamenting and communing with God. At the end of this chapter he writes:

O people of Iran! By God, in whose Power lies my soul and yours, if one day the Lord of the Age (the Twelfth Shiite Imam) were to appear and were to do anything contrary to the desires and interests of these clerics, and criticize their behaviour, these same ulama and clerics who now claim to be his vicegerents, and who pray daily for his appearance, would immediately declare him a heretic. They would shed his pure blood in the same way that Jewish divines martyred Jesus, and in the same way as Judge Sharih gave the order to kill the greatest hero of the time, the son of the Prophet, the Lord of the Age and the noblest of martyrs. It was because of this cursed cleric judge that he drank the sherbet of martyrdom.

And surely, thousands of prophets and philosophers who carried the banner of civilization and humanity were martyred at the hands of these evil-doers.[82]

Notes

1 See T. Fahd & H. Daiber, *Encyclopaedia of Islam*, 2nd edition, s.v. Ru'yā; also see Hossein Ziai in *Encylopaedia Iranica*, s.v. Dreams and Dream Interpretation. ii. In the Persian Tradition.
2 *Royâ-ye sâdeqe*, ed. B. Choubiné, no place of publication: Mard-e Emruz, 1986; Janet Afary, *The Iranian Constitutional Revolution 1906–1911: Grassroots Democracy, Social Democracy, and the Origins of Feminism*, New York: Columbia University Press, 1996, pp. 46–7.
3 On Zell-al-Soltân, his children and life at his court see Wilfrid Sparroy, *Persian Children of the Royal Family: The Narrative of an English Tutor at the Court of H.I.H. Zillu's-Sultán*, London/New York: John Lane, 1902. Sparroy writes: "The Zillu's-Sultán, while still a boy, was made the Governor-General of Isfahân; then province after province was added to his dominions, until, in the year 1886, two fifths of the whole of Persia were subject to his almost sovereign sway. From his palace in Isfahân his power extended over the districts of Gulpaigan and Khonsar, Toshagan, Irak, Isfahân, Fars, Yezd, Arabistân, Luristân, Kurdistân, Kangavar, Nehavand, Kamareh, Burujird, Kermanshâh, Asadabâd and Kezzaz." See p. 26. For a comprehensive study on Zell-al-Soltân see H.A. Walcher, *In the Shadow of the King: Zell al-Sultan and Isfahan under the Qajars*, London/New York, 2008; also V. Martin, *The Qajar Pact: Bargaining, Protest and the State in Nineteenth-Century Persia*, pp. 74–6.
4 E.G. Browne, *The Persian Revolution of 1905–1909*, London: Frank Cass & Co., 1966, p. 197. We have little information about the population of Isfahan during the Qajar period. Most of the population figures are based on European diplomats' conjectures. See Heidi Walcher in *Encyclopaedia Iranica*, s.v. Isfahan, iii. Population, iii (1). the Qajar Period, and the introduction in H.A. Walcher, *In the Shadow of the King*, but also see the memoir of Mohammad-Ali Jamâlzâde, *Sar-o tah yak karbâs yâ Esfahân-nâma*, Tehran: Âtashkade, 1955.
5 For his role during the coup of 23 June 1908 and a description of his personality see E.G. Browne, *The Persian Revolution*, p. 197.
6 J.T.P. de Bruijn, in *Encyclopaedia Iranica*, s.v. Āzād Tabrizi; also see idem, "Other Persian Quatrains in Holland: The Roseraie du Savoir of Ḥusayn-i Āzād" in *The Great 'Umar Khayyām: A Global Reception of the Rubáiyát*, ed. A. Seyed-Gohrab, Leiden: Leiden University Press, 2012, pp. 105–14. On the behaviour of Zell-al-Soltân see Yaghmâ'i, *Shahid-e râh-e âzâdi*, pp. 81–3.
7 Wilfrid Sparroy, *Persian Children of the Royal Family*, p. 161.
8 J.T.P. de Bruijn, in *Encyclopaedia Iranica*, s.v. Āzād Tabrizi; he published four anthologies of Persian poetry in French translation, two of which became very popular in the Netherlands, influencing major Dutch poets to translate and write quatrains: *Les perles de la couronne* (Paris, 1903), *Guêpes et papillons* (Paris, 1916), *La roserarie du savoir/Golzār-e ma'refat* (2 vols., Paris and Leiden, 1906) and *L'aube de l'espérance/*

Sobh-e ommid (Paris and Leiden, 1909). For a study of Hoseyn-e Âzâd's *La roserarie du savoir* see J.T.P. de Bruijn, "Other Persian Quatrains in Holland...," pp. 105–27.
9 *Ruz-nâme-ye E'temâd al-Saltaneh*, ed. I. Afshar, Tehran: 'Elmi, second print 1350/1971, p. 684; Yaghmâ'i, *Shahid-e râh-e âzâdi*, pp. 83–5; on Âqâ Najafi see V. Martin, "Aqa Najafi, Haj Aqa Nurullah, and the Emergence of Islamism in Isfahan, 1889–1908" in *Iranian Studies*, 41.2, 2008, pp. 155–72. Idem, *The Qajar Pact: Bargaining, Protest and the State in Nineteenth-Century Persia*, see chapter four, especially pp. 82–7.
10 A. Kasravi, *Târikh-e mashrute-ye Irân*, Tehran: Negâh, third print 1385/2006, p. 241. Kasravi outlines the complex situation, explaining that since Parliament considered the removal of such governors would be beneficial for the Constitutional cause, Parliament approved, and it was due to the combination of progressive clerics, intellectuals and Parliament that Zell-al-Soltân was removed from power.
11 Mohammad-Ali Jamâlzâde, *Isfahan is Half the World: Memories of a Persian Boyhood* (Translation of *Sar-o tah yek karbâs*), by W.L. Heston, Princeton: Princeton University Press, 1983, p. 59.
12 For an introduction to these movements, see *Encyclopaedia Iranica*, s.v.v. Bābism, Azali Bābism, Bāhaism, Bahā'-Allāh and 'Abd-al-Bahā. The various identities were fluid: as the Constitutional movement became opposition to Qajar rule rather than support for the rule of law, and 'Abdul-Bahâ instructed the Bâha'is to withdraw from it, some progressive intellectuals who had associated with the Bâha'is joined instead with the Azalis. There was a similar fluidity between Azalis and secular modernists. As for Sayyed Jamâl-al-Din, scholars such as E. Abrahamian, M. Bayat and L. Ridgeon refer to him as an exponent of secularism. Abrahamian refers to him as "an eloquent preacher whose audacious advocacy of secular ideas had caused his expulsion from Isfahan" (p. 79). Ridgeon states: "His criticisms were levelled at the Shi'ite clerics and Sufis. In his essay of 1900 *Lebas-e taqva* he complained of the Sufis' nomadic life and parasitical nature, as they had no jobs to procure a livelihood, and rebuked them for gambling and engaging in 'other forbidden deeds.'" See Ridgeon, *Sufi Castigator: Ahmad Kasravi and the Iranian Mystical Tradition*, London/New York: Routledge, 2006, p. 24. E. Abrahamian, *Iran between Two Revolutions*, Princeton: Princeton University Press, 1982.
13 A similar 'relevance' dynamic (as distinct from conversion) is described by Lil Osborn in *Religion and Relevance: The Bahâ'îs in Britain, 1899–1933*, Studies in the Bâbî and Bahâ'î Religions vol. 24, Kalimat Press, Los Angeles, 2014.
14 See A.L.M. Nicolas, *Massacres de Bâbis en Perse*, Paris, 1936. Also see A. Amanat, "The Historical Roots of the Persecution of Bâbis and Bâha'is in Iran" in *The Bâha'is of Iran: Socio-Historical Studies*, eds. D.P. Brookshaw and S.B. Fazel, New York, 2008, pp. 170–83, and the excellent study by S. Sadeghian, "Minorities and Foreigners in a Provincial Iranian City: Bahā'is in the Russian Consulate of Isfahan in 1903" in *Journal of Persianate Studies*, 9, 2016, pp. 107–32; also relevant is J.R.I. Cole, "Autobiography and Silence: The Early Career of Shaykh al-Ra'īs Qājār" in *Iran im 19. Jarhundert und die Entstehung der Bâha'i-Religion*, eds., J.C. Bürgel and I. Schayani, Zürich, 1998, pp. 91–126; H. Katouzian, *The Persians: Ancient, Medieval and Modern Iran*, New Haven/London: Yale University Press, 2009, pp. 176–7.
15 The dates come from E. Yaghmâ'i, *Shahid-e râh-e âzâdi*, Tehran: Tus, 1987, p. 74; this book is the most comprehensive account of Seyyed Jamâl-al-Din's life, pp. 1–75; also see N. Mozaffari. *EIr*, s.v. Jamalzadeh, Mohammad-Ali i. Life.
16 Nahid Mozaffari in *Encylcopaedia Iranica*, s.v. Jamalzadeh, Mohammad-Ali. i. Life.
17 *Isfahan is Half the World*, pp. 41–2; Persian version p. 65; also see Jamâlzâda's account in Yaghmâ'i, *Shahid-e râh-e âzâdi*, pp. 3–6 of the introduction; also see Firoozeh Kashani-Sabet, *Frontier Fictions: Shaping the Iranian Nation, 1804–1946*, London: I.B. Tauris, 2000, p. 98; on anjomans see M. Bayat, *Mysticism and Dissent: Socioreligious Thought in Qajar Iran*, Syracuse: Syracuse University Press, 1982, pp. 185–6.
18 See Janet Afary, *The Iranian Constitutional Revolution (1906–1911)*, pp. 46–7.

134   *Notes*

19 *Isfahan is Half the World*, pp. 41–2.
20 *Isfahan is Half the World*, p. 42; Persian version, p. 66. On Shuride see also Yaghmâ'i, *Shahid-e râh-e âzâdi*, p. 7; Dadkhah, "Lebas-o Taqva ...," pp. 547–558.
21 Kashani-Sabet, *Frontier Fictions*, p. 98; also see the excellent analysis of this work by M. Bayat, *Iran's First Revolution*, Oxford: Oxford University Press, 1991, pp. 64–6.
22 *Isfahan is Half the World*, p. 42; Persian version, p. 65; also see v Yaghmâ'i, *Shahid-e râh-e âzâdi*, pp. 6–12.
23 *Isfahan is Half the World*, pp. 59–60.
24 N. Mozaffari, *EIr*, s.v. Jamalzadeh, Mohammad-Ali i. Life.
25 M. Momen, "The Constitutional Movement and the Bâha'is of Iran: The Creation of an 'Enemy Within' in British" in *Journal of Middle Eastern Studies*, 2012, 39 (3), pp. 328–46; M. Bayat, *Mysticism and Dissent*, pp. 171, 179–81, where Bayat writes that Malek al-Motakallemin and Mirzâ Jahângir Khan were "secret converts."
26 E.G. Browne, *The Persian Revolution of 1905–1909*, pp. 208–9; N. Mozaffari, *EIr*, s.v. Jamalzadeh, Mohammad-Ali i. Life.
27 *Royâ-ye sâdeqe*, p. 22; on this incident see Yaghmâ'i, *Shahid-e râh-e âzâdi*, p. 27; M. Bayat, *Iran's First Revolution*, p. 111.
28 E. Abrahamian, *Iran between Two Revolutions*, p. 79.
29 *Royâ-ye sâdeqe*, p. 23; also see Browne, *The Persian Revolution*, p. 208.
30 A. Fathi, "Seyyed Jamal Vaez and the 'Aljamal' Newspaper in Iran" in *Middle Eastern Studies*, 1997, 33 (2), pp. 216–25; 'Alī-Akabr Saʿīdī Sīrjānī, in *Encyclopaedia Iranica*, s.v. Constitutional Revolution, vi. The press; E. Yaghmâ'i, *Shahid-e Âzâdi*, pp. 96–7. The first issue of the newspaper appeared on Monday 26 Moharram 1325 (Monday 11 March 1907) and the last one on Thursday 27 Rabi'-al-Thâni 1326 (Thursday 28 May 1908). In total there were thirty-six issues of the newspaper. For issues of the *al-Jamâl* see pp. 97–223. It is certainly interesting to refer to the impression Seyyed Jamâl-al-Din made on the young ʿIsâ Sadiq, who describes in his memoir how the house of Seyyed Jamâl-al-Din was only two hundred meters from their house and that Seyyed Jamâl-al-Din frequented their house to consult with his uncle and Majd al-Eslâm Kermâni, the editor of the newpaper *Nedâ-ye Watan*. Sadiq emphasizes Seyyed Jamâl-al-Din's kindness and eloquence which made a huge impression on him. See *Yâdgar-e ʿomr: khâterâti az sargozasht-e doctor ʿIsâ Sadiq ke az lahâz-e tarbiyyat sudmand tavânad bud*, vol. I, Tehran: Sherkat-e Sahâmi-ye Tabʿ-e Ketâb, 1961, pp. 20–2.
31 *The Moon of the Fourteenth Night: Being the Private Life of an Unmarried Diplomat in Persia during the Revolution*, made into a book by Eustache de Lorey and Doughlas Sladen, London: Hurst & Blackett, 1910, chapter xiii, pp. 78–90.
32 *The Moon of the Fourteenth Night*, p. viii.
33 This is a shortened version of the story of gnats and Solomon told by Jalâl al-Din Rumi in his *Mathnavi*, book iii, ed. M. Este'lâmi, Tehran: Zavvâr, 1993, p. 213, ll. 4654–63. For the Persian version of this part of the sermon see Yaghmâ'i, *Shahid-e râh-e âzâdi*, p. 110.
34 On Malek-al-Motakallemin's life see Choubiné's introduction in *Royâ-ye sâdeqe*, pp. 24–7, from which my information derives; also see M. Bayat, *Iran's First Revolution*, pp. 66–7.
35 M. Bayat, *Iran's First Revolution*, p. 66. In the same way as Wâʿez, Malek-al-Motakallemin preached in favour of progress and new sciences, turning against conservative religious scholars. As Bayat indicates, "From Tabataba'i's mosque, Malek al-Motakallemin called for the adaption of the new sciences and the modernization of education. He discussed the rise and fall of nations and the role of the clerical and temporal leaders in promoting, or obstructing, progress, holding them entirely responsible for the grandeur or decline of their society." See *Iran's First Revolution*, p. 67; also see M. Malekzâde, *Târikh-e enqelâb-e mashrutiyyat-e Irân*, Tehran: 'Elmi, 1979, pp. 429–30.
36 Browne, *The Persian Revolution*, pp. 204–5. Ahmad Kasravi refers to Mohammad-ʿAli Shah's personal hatred for Malek-al-Motakallemin. He says, "Years before the

Constitution, Malek-al-Motakallemin went to the court of Sâlâr-al-Dowle (1881–1961) in Kurdistan. When Eyn-al-Dowle, the Prime Minister (*sadr-e a'zam*), acted with enmity against Mohammad-ʿAli, wishing to strip him of the role of crown prince (valiʿahdi) and substitute one of the sons of Mozaffar-al-Din Shah, Sâlâr-al-Dowle sent Malek-al-Motakallemin to Tehran to do his best to achieve this goal. Malek-al-Motakallemin was his representative in Tehran. With the start of the Constitutional movement, Malek-al-Motakallemin forgot Sâlâr-al-Dowle and joined the Constitutionalists. But Mohammad-ʿAli had not forgotten his rancour against him." A. Kasravi, *Târikh-e mashrute*, p. 618. See also H. Katouzian, "Seyyed Hasan Taqizadeh: Three Lives in a Lifetime" in *Iran: Politics, History and Literature*, London/New York: Routledge, 2013, p. 59, where the author states, "The Shah had a deep grudge against four men in particular, Taqizadeh, Malek-al-Motakallemin, Jahangir Khan Shirazi and Seyyed Jamal Isfahani."
37 A. Kasravi, *Târikh-e mashrute*, p. 680.
38 A. Kasravi, *Târikh-e mashrute*, p. 524.
39 A. Kasravi, *Târikh-e mashrute*, p. 524.
40 E. Abrahamian, p. 78. The fifty-seven members of the Committee included "fifteen civil servants, eight educators, four translators and writers, one doctor, fourteen clergymen who had some knowledge of modern sciences, one tribal chief, three merchants, and four craftsmen."
41 As cited by Choubiné in *Royâ-ye sâdeqe*, p. 29. On Hâjj Sayyâh see M. Bayat, *Iran's First Revolution*, pp. 67–8; also see the introduction to the translation of his travels in *An Iranian in Nineteenth Century Europe: The Travel Diaries of Hâjj Sayyâh 1859–1877*, translated by Mehrbanoo Nasser Deyhim, Bethesda, MD: Ibex Publishers, 1998, pp. 15–17.
42 *Royâ-ye sâdeqe*, pp. 30–1; on Mirzâ Rezâ see H. Nâteq, *Kâr-nâme va zamâne-ye Mirzâ Rezâ Kermâni*, no place of publication, Afra, 1984, especially pp. 145–64.
43 Both of them were followers of the celebrated mojtahed Hâjji Sheykh Hâdi Najm-Âbâdi. Browne praises him for the services he rendered to the cause of liberty in Persia. He says, "He was absolutely incorruptible, and never accepted a penny from anyone. Every afternoon he used to sit on the ground outside his house, where he received people of all classes and all faiths, statesmen and scholars, princes and poets, sunnis, Shiis, Bâbis, Armenians, Jews, ʿAli-Ilahis, etc., with all of whom he discussed all sorts of topics with the utmost freedom. Though a *mujtahid*, he was at heart a free-thinker, and used to cast doubts into men's minds and destroy their belief in popular superstitions, and he was instrumental in 'awakening' a large proportion of those who afterwards became the champions of Persia's liberties." Browne, *The Persian Revolution*, p. 406. Also see p. 405.
44 N.R. Keddie, in *Encyclopaedia Iranica*, s.v. Afghānī, Jamāl-al-dīn.
45 For an English translation of Marâghe'i's work see *The Travel Diary of Ebrahim Beg by Zayn ol-ʿAbedin Maraghe'i*, trans. by James D. Clark, Costa Mesa, CA: Mazda Publishers, 2006.
46 *Royâ-ye sâdeqe*, p. 8.
47 Mohammad Hasan Khan Eʿtemâd al-Saltane, *Kh^{w}âb-e Khalse (mashhur be kh^{w}âb-nâme)*, ed. by Mahmud Katirâ'i, Tehran: Tukâ, second print 1357/1978. Also see N. Parvin in *Encyclopaedia Iranica*, s.v. Bīdārī in which he discusses three Persian newspapers published in Tehran (1907), Rasht (1920) and Kerman (1923–53) under the title *Bidâri* ('Wakefullness').
48 See A.A. Seyed-Gohrab, "Modern Persian Prose and Fiction Between 1900 and 1940" in *Literature of the Early Twentieth Century: From the Constitutional Period to Reza Shah*, ed. A.A. Seyed-Gohrab, Volume XI of *A History of Persian Literature*, London/New York: I.B. Tauris, 2015, pp. 133–60.
49 Mehrdad Kia suggests that the reference is to the Russian subjugation of Dagestan, completed in 1859. See "Constitutionalism, Economic Modernization and Islam in the

Writings of Mirza Yusef Khan Mostashar od-Dowle" in *Middle Eastern Studies*, 1994, 30 (4), pp. 752, 758.
50 *One word – Yak kaleme: 19th-century Persian Treatise Introducing Western Codified Law*, with an introduction and annotated translation by A.A. Seyed-Gohrab and S. McGlinn, Leiden: Leiden University Press, 2010, p. 7.
51 The notion of *bidâri* (lit. 'wakefulness') became very popular from this period. Nassereddin Parvin states that *bidâri* was "the name of three Persian newspapers published in Tehran (1907), Rašt (1920), and Kermān (1923–53) and also the name of several other Persian newspapers and magazines published in Iran, Europe, and the Soviet Union." See *Encyclopaedia Iranica*, s.v. Bīdārī. *Bidâri* is connected to visions of an ideal future society. There are several Utopian works in Persian and Ottoman Turkish. I am not aware of any study of the Persian Utopian works, but see Engin Kiliç, *The Balkan War (1912–1913) and Visions of the Future in Ottoman Turkish Literature*, PhD dissertation, Leiden University, 2015.
52 Nâzem-al-Eslâm Kermâni, *Târikh-e Bidâri-ye Irâniyân*, Tehran: Amir Kabir, 1999.
53 Mehdi Malekzâde, *Târikh-e Enqelâb-e mashrutiyyat-e Irân*, vol. i–iii, Tehran: Sokhan, 2004, p. 58. In Jamâlzâde's *Sar-o tah yek karbâs*, it is mentioned that the book was secretly published in 1898 in St Petersburg "with the help of Mirza Hasan Khan, who was at that time a member of the Embassy there and who later received the title Counselor of State." See Mohammad-Ali Jamâlzâde, *Isfahan is Half the World: Memories of a Persian Boyhood* (translation of *Sar-o tah yek karbâs*) by W.L. Heston, Princeton: Princeton University Press, 1983, p. 59.
54 See E. Yaghmâ'i's *Shahid-e râh-e âzâdi*, pp. 12–13, and for the text of *The True Dream* see pp. 307–37; Mehdi Malekzâde, *History of the Iranian Constitutional Revolution*, pp. 59–61.
55 See Mohammad-Ali Jamâlzâde, *Isfahan is Half the World*, p. 59.
56 Choubiné, pp. 60–1.
57 See H. Katouzian, "Satire in Persian Literature 1900–1940" in *Literature of the Early Twentieth Century from the Constitutional Period to Reza Shah*, ed. Ali-Asghar Seyed-Gohrab, London and New York: I.B. Tauris, 2015, pp. 161–239; also see Janet Afary, *The Iranian Constitutional*, p. 47; also see J. Afary, *The Iranian Constitutional Revolution (1906–1911)*, p. 47.
58 For an analytical overview see Saeed Talajooy, "A History of Iranian Drama (1850 to 1941)" in *Literature of the Early Twentieth Century: From the Constitutional Period to Reza Shah*, Volume XI, ed., Ali-Asghar Seyed-Gohrab, London/New York: I.B. Tauris, 2015, pp. 353–410; also see M.R. Ghanoonparvar in *Encyclopaedia Iranica*, s.v. Drama.
59 Mehrdad Kia, "Women, Islam and Modernity in Akhundzade's Plays and Unpublished Writings" in *Middle Eastern Studies*, 1998, 34 (3), p. 1.
60 See J.G.J. ter Haar, "Ta'ziye: Ritual Theater from Shiite Iran" in *Theatre Intercontinental: Forms, Functions, Correspondences*, ed. by C.C. Barfoot and C. Bordewijk, Amsterdam: Rodopi, 1993.
61 The fictional speaker pretends to be concealing his name, using a Persian equivalent of 'so-and-so' or John Doe.
62 The Islamic formula reads: "there is no God save God" or "Praise be to the Prophet Mohammed and his House," etc.
63 God does not appear in person. Later we will see a reference to "the Angel of the Voice," indicating that the Voice itself is an intermediary, not the voice of God in person.
64 Mirzâ Mohammad Bâqer al-Musavi Chahârsuqi al-Khwânsâri (1811–95).
65 He asks those present to call out, "May God send his peace upon the Prophet Muhammad and his family." This would occur, for example, when someone dies or is healed miraculously, hence the reference to a hospital in the following line.
66 Koran 3: 167.

Notes   137

67   At that time, equivalent to an Ayatollah today, a very high-ranking Shiah clergy.
68   That is, affecting an Arabic pronunciation.
69   Lit: Clogs are just the rind on the water melon, i.e. the part one throws away.
70   Words from a hadith said to come via Aisha. It is an expansion of Koran 18: 39.
71   Literally, several half-millions, presumably referring to monetary amounts rather than the number of messengers.
72   The meaning is approximately: the good cop and the bad cop work together. The text following this appears to be in the wrong order, or the lines of poetry have been omitted.
73   Islamic theology distinguishes the 'miracle of proof' which establishes the truth of a Prophet's calling and teachings from other miracles.
74   M. Malekzâde, *Târikh-e enqelâb-e mashrutiyyat-e Irân*, pp. 59–61.
75   Malekzâde, *Târikh-e Enqelâb*, p. 73.
76   The words are not found in this exact form in the received text of the Koran, but appear to be a citation of Koran 38: 26, influenced by 4: 58. Citations in this slightly altered form appear to be reasonably common in Iranian sources.
77   A well-known tradition, to which this author has added "male or female."
78   Koran 16: 90, but the author has replaced the verb 'command' (*amara*) with a synonym, *hakama*.
79   A widely transmitted hadith, but the author has the verb in the indicative instead of the imperative.
80   See also Malekzâde, *Târikh-e Enqelâb*, p. 129 where mention is made of Seyyed Mârbini, an eighty-year-old man, in the section on *Bâbi-koshi* or 'Bâbi-killing'; also see E. Yaghmâ'i, *Shahid-e Âzâdi*, p. 84.
81   The reference appears to be to the killing of two brothers, Mirzâ Mohammad-Hoseyn and Mirzâ Mohammad-Hoseyn Tabâtabâ'i, in Isfahan. However, the clergy who owed these two money, and brought about their deaths, was Mir-Mohammad-Hoseyn, the Emâm-Jom'e, aided by Sheykh Mohammad-Bâqir, and not Sheykh Muhammad-Taqi. The latter appears in the story only in a minor role: when the governor, Zell-al-Soltân, under pressure from the Isfahan clerics to execute the brothers immediately, prevaricated by making his executioner unavailable, Sheykh Mohammad-Taqi volunteered to execute the brothers. However, the governor eventually had the brothers executed by beheading. These facts were well known in Isfahan, so our author's confusion is telling.
82   Malekzâde, *Târikh-e Enqelâb*, pp. 59–61.

Index

'Abd-al-'Azim 17
Abil (Abel) 10
Ahmad Kasravi (1890–1946) 16
Âkhundzâde, Mirzâ Fath-'Ali (1812–1878) 18, 20
'Alâ'-al-Dowle, Mirzâ Ahmad Khan 5
'Ali b. Abi Tâlib (c. 599–661) 11
'Âmeli, Seyyed 'Isâ Sadr 3
Amin-al-Dowle, Mirzâ 'Ali Khan (1844–1904) 15, 64
Amir Afkham Qarâgozlu 6
Anjoman-e Taraqqi ('Society for Progress') 3
Anvari Sohaili 12
apostate 5, 130
Âqâ Najafi, Sheykh Mohammad-Taqi 1–4, 15, 46, 64, 128, 130
Ardâqi, Mirzâ 'Ali-Akbar Khân 15
Asadâbâdi, Seyyed Jamâl al-Din (Afghâni, 1838–1897) 17
Asadollâh Khadije Farangi 46
associations (*anjoman*s) 16, 100, 102
awakening 13, 18–19
Âzâd Tabrizi, Mirzâ Hoseyn (1854–1936) 1–2
Azalis 2, 5, 15

Babis 2–6, 11, 15, 17, 56, 133
Bâgh-e Shah 5
Bahâ'u'llâh (1817–1892) 2
Banân-al-Molk 80, 90
Behbahâni, Seyyed 'Abdollâh 5
Beheshti, Seyyed Mirzâ Nasrollâh *see* Malek-al-Motakallemin
Bibliothèque Nationale 2
Bid-Âbâdi, Seyyed Ja'far 116
blasphemy 5, 11

Cabil (Cain) 10
Chahârsuqi, Mirzâ Mohammad Hâshem 42, 46
Clothes of Piety (completed 1900) 3–4
codified laws 1, 62
company 3, 7, 100
constitution 2, 6, 13, 18
Constitutional Revolution (1905–1911) 1, 5–6, 19
constitutionalists 6, 135
Cossack 15, 78

Dabbâgh-khâna district 3
Dante Alighieri (1265–1321) 18
Dehkhodâ, 'Ali-Akbar (1879–1956) 20
Divina Comedia 18
Dowlatâbâdi, Mirzâ Yahyâ 5

E'temâd-al-Saltane, Mohammad Hasan Khan Sâni' al-Dowle, (1843–96) 2, 18
Estekhâre 17
Ezrâ'il 116

Fashâraki, Mollâ 'Ali-Akbar 94
fatwa 4, 15, 84
freedom 1, 3, 15, 20, 130, 135

Gholâm-Rezâ Khan Mohâjer 78
Gospels 10
Gowharshâd Mosque 15

Hâjj Sayyâh (1836–1925) 17
Hâjji Sâni Beyk 118
heresy 5, 15, 128, 130
Hojjat-al-Eslâm Khomâmi 15

140 Index

Hoseyn ebn ʿAli (killed 680), the third Shiite Imam 20
human rights 1

India 3, 11–12, 15, 19
Islamic Company (*Sherkat-e Eslâmi*) 3
Isrâfil 116

Jaʿfar Qoli Khan 34
Jabal ʿAmel 3
Jalil Âqâ Khan 78
Jamâlzâde, Mohammad-ʿAli (1892–1997) 2–5, 19–20
Jesus 10, 131
Joséph Desirée Tholozan (1820–1897) 1
justice 1, 13–14, 26, 28, 36, 42, 44, 50, 68, 70, 76, 78, 84, 86, 92, 94, 96, 104, 106, 112, 114, 116, 118, 129–130

Kalila and Dimnah 11
Kâzeruni, Mohammad Hoseyn 3
Kermâni, Âqâ Khân, Mirzâ ʿAbd al-Hoseyn (1854–1896) 5, 18
Kermâni, Hâjj Mirzâ Ahmad (Majd al-Eslâm) 1, 3, 16–17
Kermâni, Mirzâ Rezâ 17
Kermâni, Nâzem-al-Eslâm 19
Kh^wâb-e khalse, (known as *Kh^wâb-nâme* 'Record of a Dream') 18

Lebanon 3
lullaby 18
luti 4

Mahallâti, Hâjj Mohammad-ʿAli *see* Hâjj Sayyâh
Majlis 13–14
Maktubât 18
Malek-al-Motakallemin 1, 3, 5, 14–16, 19, 135
Malekzâde 19, 128–130
Masâlek al-Mohsenin 18
Mâzanderâni, Seyyed Taqi 46
Mecca 15, 72, 74
Men al-Khalq ela al-haqq (*From People to the Truth*) 15
messianic movement 2
Mirzâ ʿAbd-al-Wahhâb 84, 86, 88, 94

Mirzâ Bâqer Khan 86, 94, 108, 110, 112, 114
Mirzâ Fath-ʿAli Khan 100, 102, 104
Mirzâ Habibollâh Khan 64
Mirzâ Jahângir Khan (d. 1908) 4, 15–16
Mohammad-ʿAli Shah (1872–1925) 5–6, 15
Mortazâ-Qoli Khan Wakil-al-Molk 17
Moshir-al-Molk 80, 90, 110, 112
Mostashâr-al-Dowle, Mirzâ Yusof Khan (d. 1895)1, 18
Mozaffar-al-Din Shah (1853–1907) 1, 15
Mozaffar-al-Molk 6, 80

Najm-Âbâdi, Sheykh Hâdi 15
Naqneh, Mulla Mohammad 34
Nâser-al-Din Shah (1831–1896) 1–2, 17, 90
Nâyeb-al-Saltane 2
Nâzem-al-Khalvat, Mirzâ Mohammad Khan 26
Neyriz 17
novels 12, 20

parliament 5–6, 15–16
Parsees 15
passion plays (*taʿziyye*) 20

Qâʿâni (Persian poet, c. 1807–1853) 78
Qanbar, the black Ethiopian servant 20

rebellion 32, 34
Rizi, Sheykh Mortezâ 76
Rokn-al-Molk 86, 94, 96, 98, 102, 114
Roshdiyye school 15
*rowzeh-khân*s 4
Rumi, Jalâl al-Din (1207–1273) 14, 80, 92, 130
Russians 5–6, 19

Saʿdi of Shiraz (d. 1292) 82, 110, 112, 124, 126
Sabz-i-Maydan 7
Sad Khetâbe 18
Sadr-al-Mohaqqeqin ('Chief among Scholars') 4
Sâheb-Zamâni, Seyyed Hasan 17
Sahrâ-ye mahshar (*The Plain of Resurrection*) 20

Sârem-al-Dowle 80, 90, 110
Sar-o tah yek karbâs 19
Satan 1, 54, 130
Sayyid Abu Ja'far 24, 116, 118
scales of justice 26, 28, 42, 50, 70, 76, 78, 84, 94, 104, 106, 116, 118
School of Chahâr Bâgh 60
School of Mulla 'Abdolah 60
School of Nim Avard Kaseh Garan 60
Sepahsâlâr school 16
Seyyed Abu Tâlib 116, 118
Shams-Âbâdi, Hâjji Seyyed Abd al-Wahhâb 94
Sharafejân, Mirzâ Hâshem 64
Shiite saints 20
Shirâzi, Seyyed 'Ali-Mohammad (the Bâb, executed in 1850) 2
Shuride of Shiraz 3
Siyâhat-nâme Ebrâhim Beg 18
Sladen, Doughlas 6
Sobh-e Azal (1830–1912) 2
Sulayman (King Solomon) 14, 134
Soltân Mas'ud Mirzâ *see* Zell-al-Soltân
Sur-e Esrâfil 5, 15

Tabâtabâ'i, Seyyed Mohammad 5, 15
Talebov, 'Abd-al-Rahim (1834–1911) 19
Târikh-e Bidâri-ye Irâniyân (*History of the Awakening of the Iranians*) 19
textile company 3
tobacco 7, 100

ulamâ 8, 28, 30, 32, 36, 44, 46, 48, 62, 74, 76, 84, 100, 128, 131

Valmont, Edouard 6

Wâ'ez Esfahâni, Seyyed Jamâl-al-Din (or Hamadâni, 1862–1908) 1, 3–13, 16, 19–20, 134
Wakil-al-Molk, Mortazâ-Qoli Khân 17
World Exhibition (Paris 1898) 2

Yek Kalame (*One Word*) 18

Zell-al-Soltân, ('The Shadow of the King') 1–3, 15, 19, 34, 40, 66, 76, 96, 98, 100, 102, 104, 108, 110, 132, 137
Zeyn-al-'Âbedin Marâghe'i 18

Taylor & Francis eBooks

Helping you to choose the right eBooks for your Library

Add Routledge titles to your library's digital collection today. Taylor and Francis ebooks contains over 50,000 titles in the Humanities, Social Sciences, Behavioural Sciences, Built Environment and Law.

Choose from a range of subject packages or create your own!

Benefits for you
- Free MARC records
- COUNTER-compliant usage statistics
- Flexible purchase and pricing options
- All titles DRM-free.

Benefits for your user
- Off-site, anytime access via Athens or referring URL
- Print or copy pages or chapters
- Full content search
- Bookmark, highlight and annotate text
- Access to thousands of pages of quality research at the click of a button.

REQUEST YOUR FREE INSTITUTIONAL TRIAL TODAY

Free Trials Available
We offer free trials to qualifying academic, corporate and government customers.

eCollections – Choose from over 30 subject eCollections, including:

Archaeology	Language Learning
Architecture	Law
Asian Studies	Literature
Business & Management	Media & Communication
Classical Studies	Middle East Studies
Construction	Music
Creative & Media Arts	Philosophy
Criminology & Criminal Justice	Planning
Economics	Politics
Education	Psychology & Mental Health
Energy	Religion
Engineering	Security
English Language & Linguistics	Social Work
Environment & Sustainability	Sociology
Geography	Sport
Health Studies	Theatre & Performance
History	Tourism, Hospitality & Events

For more information, pricing enquiries or to order a free trial, please contact your local sales team:
www.tandfebooks.com/page/sales

 Routledge Taylor & Francis Group | The home of Routledge books

www.tandfebooks.com